Conversations of the Crucifixion

Darrius Jerome Gourdine,
DJG Enterprises

DJG
Enterprises

Conversations of the Crucifixion

Darrius Jerome Gourdine,
DJG Enterprises

Foreword by Elder R. Kevin Matthews

Foreword by Reverend Dr. Maurice J. Nutt

© Copyright 2014, Darrius Jerome Gourdine. All rights reserved.

No part of this book may be reproduced, stored in a retrieval system, or transmitted in any form by any means, electronic, mechanical, photocopying, recording, or otherwise without prior written permission, except in the case of brief quotations embodied in critical articles and reviews.

Cover Design: Victoria Fleary

Book layout and design: Norman Rich

Author photography by Darnell Gourdine Photography

For book signings and speaking engagements, send all inquiries to info@crucifixionconversations.com.

All scriptural references are taken from the New King James version of the Holy Bible.

www.crucifixionconversations.com

ISBN: 0-9755660-2-4

Dedication

This book is respectfully dedicated to the memories of my grandparents, Reverends John and Annie Dupree. Thank you for the many prayers and Bible lessons over the course of my life. Thank you for being pillars of the community and of the church. Thank you for setting a shining example for our family and for the legacy you've left for us. Thank you for teaching your children, grandchildren and great grandchildren who Jesus is. Rest in Jesus.

Foreword

In 2010, I clearly heard the voice of the Lord in prayer. His instruction for me was to put together an illustrated sermon where seven of the items or individuals used to crucify Jesus are speaking in first person.

Those seven items and individuals were: the Roman soldiers, the whip, the hammer, the nails, the crown of thorns, the cross, and the spear that pierced Him. They would each speak and give their personal testimony of the event of the crucifixion of Jesus and the impression it made on them. I immediately reached out to Darrius Jerome Gourdine and asked that he write the script. He masterfully executed the dialogue in first person from each of the six items and the soldiers. The sermon was impactful and powerful!

One year later, Darrius approached me and let me know that the Lord had placed it on his heart to transform the sermon written for the stage to a book. In order to do this, many more items and individuals would have to be added. After two years of prayer, research and writing, I am proud that he has accomplished the task that God has placed before him.

Conversations of the Crucifixion is a powerful piece in which you, the reader, will see the crucifixion of our Lord in a different way. Everyone has their own interpretation of the crucifixion. How many of us however have wondered what the cross would say if it could speak? What the whip or the tomb would say? What about the angel at the tomb or even the Garden of Gethsemane? This book is Darrius' interpretation of the answer to these questions. I highly recommend *Conversations of the Crucifixion* to any child of God who respects the work that Jesus did on the cross and wants to see that work from many different perspectives.

Elder R. Kevin Matthews

Evangel Cathedral

Foreword

Were you there when they crucified my Lord?
Were you there when they crucified my Lord?
Oh, Oh sometimes it causes me to tremble,
tremble, tremble.
Were you there when they crucified my Lord?
— African American Spiritual

Darrius Jerome Gourdine masterfully takes the reader on a transforming and provocative journey that transports you back in time to that fateful yet redemptive day and place where Jesus hung on a cross and died.

There were few who dared to remain. Fear, insecurity, uncertainty, guilt, and worst of all indifference scattered many from the Roman execution site outside of Jerusalem called "Golgotha" – the place of skulls.

Yet by virtue of Darrius' spiritual imagination and keen creativity, you revisit and rediscover new insights and first person testimonies that enable you to revision and reclaim anew the place and events that wrought your salvation. *Conversations of the Crucifixion* beckons you to remain at the foot of the cross to see and to experience what those who were there witnessed.

In his unique, innovative writing style, Darrius

Jerome Gourdine not only offers first person accounts of Mary Magdalene, Peter, Pontius Pilate, and Judas, but gives voices to the unsuspecting inanimate objects as well! You will hear the first person stories of the nails, the hammer, the whip, the spear, the crown of thorns and even the cross itself. Undeniably these objects were not only present at the crucifixion of Jesus but were active participants in His brutal execution.

You may have thought you knew the story surrounding the events of Calvary; however, *Conversations of the Crucifixion* will make you think again. I caution you not to casually read this book. It is not casual reading – it is a spiritual re-awakening that demands that you savor it, meditate on it and enter into dialogue with it. In so doing, you can steadfastly proclaim, "Yes, I was there when they crucified my Lord!"

Reverend Dr. Maurice J. Nutt
Catholic Evangelist / Author / Motivational Speaker
Chicago, IL

Contents

Dedication	4
Foreword	5
Table of Contents	9
Introduction	11
The Palm Branch	13
The Towel	17
The Bread	21
The Wine	25
Garden of Gethsemane	29
The Blood	33
Judas Iscariot	39
The Roman Soldier	53
Peter	59
Pontius Pilate	77
The Whipping Post	89
The Whip	93
The Crown of Thorns	97
Simon of Cyrene	103
The Cross	111

The Sign on the Cross	117
The Hammer	123
The Nails	129
The Sponge	137
The Spear	141
Gestas Thief	147
Dismas the Thief	157
The Tomb	167
Mary Magdalene	177
The Stone	189
The Angels at the Tomb	193
Cleopas	199
Thomas	213
Two Men in White Robes	225
Epilogue	229

Introduction

Many people came into contact with Jesus throughout the ordeal of His arrest, trial, scourging, sentencing, crucifixion, resurrection, and ascension. As believers and followers of the crucifixion story, we see this chain of events from a variety of angles and perspectives.

In this book, *Conversations of the Crucifixion*, I have attempted to give the perspective of the individual or object in contact with Jesus. The nails are speaking. *If the nails could speak, what would they say?* The hammer is speaking. *If the hammer could speak, what would it say?* The cross is speaking. *If the cross could speak, what would it say?*

This is the premise of this book and I pray that you find it as enlightening of a read as I found it to write. I pray that God blesses you as you see His sacrifice from a different perspective.

Darrius Jerome Gourdine

Jesus feeds the multitude

The Palm Branch

> *"The next day a great multitude that had come to the feast, when they heard that Jesus was coming to Jerusalem, took branches of palm trees and went out to meet Him, and cried out: 'Hosanna! Blessed is He who comes in the name of the LORD! The King of Israel!'"*
> — John 12:12-13

"I am the Palm Branch!"

I was used to pave the way when Jesus entered Jerusalem to a parade of people praising him as king. As he drew close to the city, many in the town became excited, as they knew of him from the miracles he had performed. Jesus had healed the sick and had raised a man from the dead.

He had turned water into wine and even walked on top of water. He is an amazing man and the people are aware that he was coming to town. They were so excited that they began tearing me out of the trees and lying me on the road before him.

When I heard that King Jesus was entering the city, I was excited to see him again. The news about him traveled so fast that I heard people talking about him daily. It was very common for me to provide shade for someone who sat and spoke about the wonders that Jesus could perform and his claim to be the Son of God. Although I had seen him in the city several times, it was always good to see him and the attraction that he generated.

This day was different however, as people were more excited than usual to see him. The town emptied as news came that he was at the city limits. Thousands of people lined the streets to get a close look or a touch from him. The scene was pandemonium. A few people climbed the trees to get a better look, or so I thought. I quickly found out that they were not interested in a better look, they were interested in me! I've never been the center of attraction! I've never felt such love and respect! People seemed generally interested in me! Thousands of people! All climbing trees! Pulling me! Snatching at me! Calling one another to distribute me! They began pulling me out of the trees one at a time and then bunches at a time. Soon the scene became frenzied! I was everywhere! Everyone wanted to have me. Everyone wanted to wave me.

They then began laying me on the road ahead of the donkey that Jesus was riding on. Quickly, I covered the entire entryway. You could barely see the road for the sake of so many branches that had been laid down. It was as jubilant a celebration as Jerusalem had seen in years. There were palm branches waving everywhere by thousands of people and palm branches lining the road that Jesus rode in on. What a spectacular sight!

Even with all the commotion, excitement and enthusiasm that took place, there were some who were not excited about the events and what was happening. The Pharisees were not only void of excitement, but they were rather upset. They bitterly complained about the common people waving me as Jesus entered. The Pharisees and Sadducees are well versed in the Law of Moses where it specifically states, "And you shall take for yourselves on the first day the fruit of beautiful trees, branches of palm trees, the boughs of leafy trees, and willows of the brook; and you shall rejoice before the LORD your God for seven days." This instruction is given for The Feast of Tabernacles. Palm branches are only to be waved during this feast, not the current feast which is The Passover Feast. The Pharisees and Sadducees are upset that I am being waved at the wrong feast.

They are also quite upset that the people are calling Jesus a king. They know that the Romans are in power. If the Romans believe that the Jews are establishing a government with a king in command, they would suspect a military strike. The Pharisees and Sadducees do not want to lose the amount of power they are allowed to have under Roman rule and authority. Therefore, they vehemently oppose the people calling Jesus a king and waving palm branches in front of Him.

They begin going through the crowd and snatching me from the hands of the people. They angrily tell the people to stop waving me and to put me down. They don't realize that waving me towards Jesus is much more than just taking me from a tree or the observance of the wrong feast. I represent something a lot more substantial than that. If you look at the walls of the temple of Solomon, you will see that there are two objects carved into the gold walls. The two objects are angels and palm branches. The angels are carved there because their purpose is to worship God in the beauty of His holy presence. I am carved there because my purpose is to represent the praise of His people. When you take me away from the people, you take their praise away. The people were influenced to stop praising Jesus as king because I was taken from them.

There is reason to rejoice however for it was prophesied by John; written in his book called Revelations, "After these things I looked, and behold, a great multitude which no one could number, of all nations, tribes, peoples, and tongues, standing before the throne and before the Lamb, clothed with white robes, with palm branches in their hands, and crying out with a loud voice, saying, "Salvation belongs to our God who sits on the throne, and to the Lamb!'" The people will receive me again and be able to praise!

God's children don't have to wait until that day to praise him. God gave his children two hands, each with a palm. Hands can be lifted in adoration. Hands can be clasped together in prayer. Hands can be waved in worship. Hands can be clapped in praise. I am a palm branch. I represent the praise of God. I was waved in the past and I will be waved in the kingdom to come.

The Towel

> *"After that, he poured water into a basin and began to wash his disciples' feet, drying them with the towel that was wrapped around him."*
> — John 13:5

"I am the Towel!"

I was used by Jesus to wash the feet of his disciples at the Passover Feast. Little is known about me, but I am a significant part of the life of Jesus and the lessons He passed on to his followers.

It was a well-known Jewish custom that the least important person in attendance would wash the feet of the others in the room. The towel, basin and water were left by the door so the act could be initiated by the least person, usually a servant, once he entered. In likewise fashion, I was waiting by the door for someone to pick me up and start this ritual. I watched as each of the disciples passed by me. Each thought himself too high or valuable for such a menial act. No one picked me up. No one looked my way. No one considered me. I felt useless. I felt overlooked. Not only was I overlooked but I now feel like the least important element of the feast. Everyone respects the Passover lamb. People are consciously aware of the unleavened bread and the wine. No one takes the time to consider me. Everyone passes by. Each of the twelve, along with Jesus, takes his place at the table for the Passover meal.

Towards the end of the meal, Jesus does an unusual thing. He stands and takes his clothes off. He walks to me and picks me up. He wraps me around his waist. He takes the basin and fills it with water. He walks toward Bartholomew and kneels in front of him. He plunges me into the water and uses me to clean the dirt off of his feet. He removes dirt from this man's feet and then moves to the next man. He does the same; plunges me into the water, wipes the man's feet and removes all of the dirt. He does this to John, Thomas, Matthew and Luke. He does it for Phillip and Thaddeus.

As he kneels in front of Peter, Peter pulls his feet away. Peter then asks Lord, "Are you going to wash my feet?"

Jesus replied, "You do not realize now what I am doing, but later you will understand." Peter does not want Jesus to wash his feet and demands that He not do it. He goes so far as to say that Jesus will never wash his feet. Jesus then says, "Unless I wash you, you have no part with me." Peter then allows Jesus to wash him yet he still doesn't quite understand what Jesus is doing or why he did it.

Jesus has come to remove the sin from all believers. He has come to transform unclean people and make them clean. He washes the filth and dirt away. He has no problem mingling in the dirt. Instead of insisting the sinner walk into the temple to be made clean, Jesus instead went to the home of the sinner.

He went to the gatherings of the sinners. He went to unclean individuals and made them clean.

The Pharisees brought a woman to Jesus who they caught in the act of adultery. They threw her to the ground and asked Jesus' opinion on the matter. They were attempting to set Jesus up for they did not bring the man who committed the act with her as the law required. The set up was that they wanted him to condemn her to death. The Law of Moses stated that this woman was to be stoned for committing adultery.

When asked his opinion, Jesus calmly knelt down and began to mingle in the dirt. They continued questioning until He rose and declared "Let he who is without sin, cast the first stone." One by one the Pharisees dropped their stones and walked away. All the while, Jesus was writing in the dirt. Once they had all left, he stands and faces the woman. She did not know what he would then say or do. He may have stoned her himself. He may have tried to use her as other men probably had. Instead he asks her, "Where are your accusers? Has no one condemned you?"

"No one sir," she says in reply.

"I don't condemn you either," he says. "Go forth and sin no more." He has forgiven her of her sins without condemnation. Jesus did not come into the world to condemn the world, but so that the world through him might be saved.

Jesus plunges me into the water again. He rings me out and kneels in front of another. This one's name is Judas Iscariot. Jesus looks into his eyes. He then looks deeper; past his eyes and looks into his heart. satan has already entered the heart of Judas. Jesus sees him. Jesus looks directly into the eyes of satan.

He then takes me and begins to wipe the feet of Judas. He removes all of the dirt from the feet of Judas. He removes all of the muck and grime from his feet. He cleans his feet thoroughly. Jesus shows that his believers have the power to wish well upon those that mean them harm. This is a powerful act that Jesus' believers can learn a great deal from. Even though satan is planning Jesus' demise, Jesus still washes the feet of Judas.

When he had finished washing their feet, he put on his clothes and returned to his place at the table. He then says, "Do you understand what I have done for you? You call me Teacher and 'Lord, and rightly so, for that is what I am. Now that I, your Lord and Teacher, have washed your feet, you also should wash one another's feet. I have set you an example that you should do as I have done for you. Very truly I tell you, no servant is greater than his master, nor is a messenger greater than the one who sent him. Now that you know these things, you will be blessed if you do them."

Jesus has taught a tremendous lesson; to be great in his kingdom is to be a servant to his people. He instructs that the first shall be last and the last shall be first. Believers should never think that they are above one another. He knelt down and washed feet. He removed dirt. He didn't cut the feet or condemn the sinner. Instead, he simply removed the sin and made the sinner clean.

The Bread

"While they were eating, Jesus took bread, and when He had given thanks, He broke it and gave it to his disciples, saying, 'Take and eat; this is my body.'"
— Matthew 26:26

"I am the Bread!"

I am a part of the Passover Feast and have become symbolic in the Communion sacrament. I am half of the elements, as I coexist with the wine. Both represent an important aspect of Jesus. I represent His body and the wine represents His blood.

During the meal, I am waiting to be used. I patiently sit on the table until the meal is fully consumed. I begin to think I would not be used by anyone, much less Jesus himself. At the moment when I had given up hope as to whether or not I would be important, useful, or utilized, *Jesus takes me.*

I immediately become overwhelmed at the thought of being taken by Jesus. I know that I will be used for some divine service. I cannot state what the divine service is, for I do not know. The thought of being taken however has filled me with excitement and joy. To be taken is to be set aside or consecrated for service.

Jesus takes me. Jesus breaks me. Jesus gives me.

Then Jesus does something that I wasn't expecting; He breaks me in half. He does this to symbolize his body, which will be broken as he is being crucified. In a matter of hours, he will be severely beaten. He will be punched, kicked, whipped and nailed. They will thrust a spear into his side. More painful will be the accusations and curses hurled at him. His body will be broken.

Jesus takes me. Jesus breaks me. Jesus gives me.

Jesus gives me to his friends. He invites them all to take part and receive me. I am passed from one man to the next. Each time, a piece of me is taken and consumed.

Jesus takes me. Jesus breaks me. Jesus gives me.

By the time I return to the hands of Jesus, I recognize that I am no longer my former self. I have been greatly used by God. I have become one of the greatest symbols in the lives of the followers of Jesus, yet I am only a shell of whom and what I once was.

Jesus takes me. Jesus breaks me. Jesus gives me.

During that seemingly simple act, I was used to transform the Feast of the Passover into something entirely different. I was used by God in a way that I was not aware. On this night, I was transformed from the unleavened bread of the Passover Feast to the bread of the communion. I became known by the followers of Jesus everywhere as the symbol of his body being broken during the act of the crucifixion. Not only that, I became an example of the manner in which God uses vessels. A seed is a vessel. A seed has to be taken and planted, it has to break out of its outer shell, and it must be given away as fruit in order to fulfill God's purpose for it. A person is a vessel. A person is taken aside by God, they will go through a breaking period, and then they are given to the service of God's people to fulfill God's purpose for them.

I was greatly used by God in a simple act. *Jesus took me. Jesus blessed me. Jesus broke me. Jesus gave me.*

The Holy Communion

The Wine

"Then he took a cup, and when he had given thanks, he gave it to them, saying, 'Drink from it, all of you. This is my blood of the covenant, which is poured out for many for the forgiveness of sins. I tell you, I will not drink from this fruit of the vine from now on until that day when I drink it new with you in my Father's kingdom.'"
— Matthew 26:27-28

"I am the Wine!"

I am a very recognizable element in what is practiced as the communion sacrament. I represent the blood of Jesus that is poured out for the forgiveness of the sin of mankind. When Jesus passed the wine to his disciples during the Passover meal, he mentions that I am the blood of the new covenant.

In the old covenant, the high priest would take the blood of an animal into the tabernacle. Once he entered the tabernacle, with the blood in his possession, he was able to go into covenant with the Father on behalf of the people. In like fashion, Jesus took his own blood into the tabernacle in heaven. Jesus entered with his own blood on behalf of the people. His act allows the sins of the people to be forgiven. I represent the blood of Jesus.

On the night that Jesus was betrayed, I was

poured into four different cups as is the custom of the Passover Feast. Each of the cups represent one of the four "I wills" of God. When God gave Moses the instructions for the first Passover, He said "I will" four separate times. For this, the custom is to celebrate these sayings of God and represent them in four cups of wine.

In the book of Exodus, God says, "Therefore, say to the Israelites: I am the LORD, and I will bring you out from under the burden of the Egyptians. I will rid you of their bondage, and I will redeem you with an outstretched arm and with mighty acts of judgment. I will take you as my own people, and I will be your God."

God says "I will" four times. He says, "I will bring you out, I will rid you of their bondage, I will redeem you, and I will take you as my own people and be your God." These are the four "I wills" of God.

I am poured into the first cup which is called The Cup of Separation. My cup has this name for the first "I will" in which God says "I will bring you out." When the Children of Israel were in Egypt, they were enslaved and under tremendous burden. God promised to bring them out from this horrible situation. In doing so, God has separated them from the place where they were. He has delivered them.

I am poured into the second cup which is called The Cup of Blessing. My cup has this name for the second "I will" in which God says "I will rid you of their bondage." The Children of Israel were free from Egypt but they were still slaves in their minds.

God blessed the Israelites by destroying their slave mentality and their old way of thinking.

I am poured into the third cup which is called The Cup of Redemption. My cup has this name for the third "I will" in which God says "I will redeem you." To redeem is to rescue by paying a price. The price that Jesus paid to rescue mankind was death. I represent the blood that has rescued mankind.

I am poured into the fourth cup which is called The Cup of Acceptance. My cup has this name for the fourth "I will" in which God says "I will take you to me as my own people and I will be your God." This cup is for those who will accept Jesus into their lives and become believers. As they have accepted Him, this cup is for them and I am poured into it accordingly.

Near the conclusion of the Passover meal, Jesus bypasses the first cup, The Cup of Separation. He bypasses the second cup, The Cup of Blessing. He picks up the third cup, The Cup of Redemption. He passes The Cup of Redemption to His disciples and says "Drink from it, all of you. This is my blood of the covenant, which is poured out for many for the forgiveness of sins." I am then passed to each of the disciples in the room inside The Cup of Redemption. I am passed around. I am swirling in the cup. Each man drinks and the last man hands the cup back to Jesus.

Jesus then picks up the fourth cup, The Cup of Acceptance and says "I tell you, I will not drink from this fruit of the vine from now on until that day when I drink it new with you in my Father's kingdom." He places the fourth cup back down without drinking from it or passing it around. Understanding that everyone will not accept him, Jesus vows to not drink from The Cup of Acceptance. He says that he will not drink me from this cup until he does it in his Father's kingdom. The only people allowed in the Father's kingdom are those who have accepted Jesus. Jesus and all who believe in Him will drink me from The Cup of Acceptance then.

    I am the wine. I represent the blood of Jesus which was shed for the remission of sins. During the sacrament of Communion, I am passed as the third cup, The Cup of Redemption. Just as Jesus has passed this cup to his disciples, I am passed during Communion today. Just as each person in attendance with Jesus was redeemed because of the wine in the cup; those who partake in Communion are rescued by the price that Jesus paid with His blood.

Garden of Gethsemane

"Then Jesus went with his disciples to a place called Gethsemane, and he said to them, 'Sit here while I go over there and pray.'"
— Matthew 26:36

"I am the Garden of Gethsemane!"

I sit at the foot of the Mount of Olives in Jerusalem. I am most famous as the place where Jesus prayed the night he was arrested, the day before his death. Since that night I have been spoken of, yet misunderstood for centuries. I've become one of the most famous gardens in history.

My name, Gethsemane, is derived from two words; gath, which means wine-press, and sheme, meaning grease, especially a liquid such as olive oil. When an olive is placed into an olive press, it is pressured to the point of breaking. It does not break, yet the pressure is intense. The purpose of applying this type of pressure is to squeeze the olive enough that all of the oil inside of it flows out.

On the night that Jesus entered, he was accompanied by three disciples; Peter, James and John, whom he asked to stay awake and pray. He moved a stone's throw away from them, where he felt overwhelming sadness and anguish. He begins to feel the pressure as he starts to pray. I listen intently as Jesus prays. This is the man who taught others to pray. Now, he is praying for himself and he sounds nervous. He asks if this cup can pass from him. He sounds as if he is under tremendous pressure. As the olive feels pressure in the press, so does Jesus.

After an hour of continuous prayer, he gets up to check on the three disciples. They are all asleep. He wakes them up and warns them to stay awake and pray. He returns to his place of prayer.

This second prayer feels more intense than the first, even though the words are similar. As the olive feels pressure in the press, so does Jesus. He prays, "My Father, if it is possible, let this cup pass me by. Nevertheless, let it be as you, not I, would have it. Not my will, but Yours be done." His body is now trembling and he is sweating. I've never seen nor heard a man pray like this before. He prays continuously for yet another hour. His Father never answers him.

Jesus returns to the three and like the first time, they are sound asleep. He tells them that the spirit is willing but the flesh is weak. Like the first time, he instructs them to pray. He wishes to pray once more.

He returns to the place where he had been praying. He falls upon his face and says the prayer that he had been previously praying. This time however, he is sweating profusely. His garment becomes drenched with sweat. He looks as if he has been crying, yet it is sweat. Sweat drops are falling from his head, as if it were great drops of blood. As the olive feels pressure in the press, so does Jesus.

As the olive is pressed, it is only when it gets to the point of breaking that the oil flows out of it. Intense pressure is what causes the oil to flow. In the scriptures, oil is a representation of the anointing . In order for the anointing to flow from a person, intense pressure is applied to the person's life. The olive oil is representative of the anointing.

In Exodus chapter 30, God gives Moses the ingredients for the anointing oil which will be used to anoint the members of the priesthood. Of the five ingredients mentioned, a hin of olive oil is the fifth ingredient. The olive oil constitutes the final ingredient in making the oil of anointing. Jesus' anointing could now flow because he allowed his flesh and soul to be troubled in prayer. As the olive felt pressure in the press, so did Jesus. The pressure created a flow of his anointing and enabled him to embrace his final earthly destiny.

The Transfiguration of Jesus Christ

The Blood

"For this is my blood of the new testament, which is shed for many for the remission of sins."
— Matthew 26:28

"I am the blood!"

I exist with Jesus in both the spiritual world and the physical world. In the spiritual realm, I am the blood of Jesus through the bloodline of his earthly ancestors. I came through Adam, the son of God, and on through Seth his son. The lineage of sons continued through Noah and onto Abraham.

I flowed through his son Isaac and his son Jacob. I traveled through Judah, of the sons of Israel. I passed through son after son after son. I passed through Boaz, who married Ruth. I passed through their son Obed, who begot Jesse who begot David. From David I went forth and flowed through King Solomon, and then King Rehoboam. I flowed through Kings Uzziah and Hezekiah. I flowed all the way down the family line through Josiah, Shealtiel, Mathan, Jacob and Joseph, the husband of Mary. This is where I exist with Jesus in the spirit realm. It is the spirit realm because Joseph was not allowed to know his wife Mary. Therefore, none of his blood was able to enter the body of the baby in Mary's body. Yet we know him as the seed of Abraham, the root of Jesse and the son of David.

I also exist with Jesus in the physical world. In the physical realm, I am the blood of Jesus that was poured out on the cross. By Jesus going to the cross to be crucified for sin, it was the representation of the sacrificial lamb in the tabernacle of Moses that was killed for the sins of the children of Israel. The blood of the sacrificial lamb was poured on the altar to atone for the sins of the people. The blood of Jesus was poured in like manner. Therefore, Jesus had to be birthed from the womb of a woman in order to have me in His body to pour out through the act of the crucifixion. I exist with Jesus in both the spiritual world and the physical world.

I silently pumped through the arteries and veins of Jesus and patiently awaited my time. I knew my destiny. I knew my calling. Jesus was born to die; specifically he was born to bleed. I knew that my days were numbered from the first day he entered the earth realm as a human. Yet I patiently waited, never revealing my purpose or the secret to the strength of Jesus. The book of Leviticus declares that the life of the flesh is in the blood. Jesus was born as a baby to give his life for all mankind. He was born to give me; his blood; his life.

When Jesus entered the temple as a young boy and astonished the scholars, I was there with him. When Jesus learned carpentry from Joseph, I was running through him. When Jesus stepped to the Jordan River to be baptized by John, I was pumping in and out of his heart.

After being baptized, he was directed by the Spirit to fast and pray. Jesus fasted 40 days. Being in a weakened state, satan approached him with three temptations. Each temptation was resisted by Jesus until satan would flee to return another time. Upon satan's return, he brought an army of demons. These spirits would tempt Jesus every day through his three years of ministry on earth. They approached him from every direction, on each day, within each hour and utilizing each minute. Every opportunity they could, they did. Jesus was never afforded an opportunity to retreat or relax from the pressure of the spirit realm. He never wavered, yet remained steadfast toward his mission. These spirits never were able to securely occupy Jesus' body. They surrounded him but never oppressed him. They tried to leap on him from every direction and failed every time. He never showed a sign of weakness until the night he was arrested in the Garden of Gethsemane.

After Jesus prayed earnestly on three separate occasions, soldiers and guards came to seize Him. Once they approached, a violent fight ensued and guards began to beat Jesus. Jesus was punched in the lip, hit in the eye, and smacked in the face. At some point his skin was broken and I showed forth. The very second I came through his skin, one of the spirits landed on him. This spirit sent by Satan had been trying to occupy Jesus for three years and never was able to do so. Yet the second I broke out of his body, the spirit landed on Jesus. As I started to pour out, another spirit landed on Jesus. Then a third spirit landed. Then a fourth landed. At first they rushed Jesus one at a time. Then several landed on him. My secret was revealed; I was the key! I was the protection! I am the life! Once the secret was revealed, the influence to beat Jesus mercilessly became the mission of Satan and the rebellious spirits.

The more they beat him, the more he bled. The more he bled, the more spirits leaped on him. He grew weaker in both realms. He grew weaker in the spirit realm, for now he is carrying the sin of mankind. He now carried the spirit of fear. He now carried the spirit of greed. He now carried the spirit of lust. He now carried the spirit of envy. He also grew weaker in the physical realm. As he lost blood, he grew tired and cold. He grew weak as he carried a cross. I exist with Jesus in both the spiritual world and the physical world.

By the time Jesus hung on the cross, he had lost so much of me and exchanged me for so much sin that his Father forsook him. Jesus cried out "My God! My God! Why have you forsaken me?" Jesus' pain of being forsaken is so excruciating that this is the first time Jesus refers to his Father by the title My God, instead of his Father in heaven.

As Jesus hung on the cross that afternoon, I continued to pour from him. I poured from his head, his hands, his face, his neck, his shoulders, his back, his stomach, his legs and his feet. He held on to what little life he had left in him through me. His life on earth was quickly coming to an end as I seeped out. For without me, a body has no life. The life of the flesh is in the blood. Before he could declare that his work was finished, he had to get all of me out. In the spirit realm, I became an exchange for the sin of man. When a man or woman accepts this sacrificial act of Jesus, their sin leaves them in the spirit and lands on Jesus on the cross. In exchange, the blood of Jesus leaves his body and lands on that man or woman. This happens in an instant and spans time. This is my purpose: to leave the body of Jesus as an exchange for the sin of a believer.

This is why it was imperative that he got all of me out. If there was any blood left inside of his body, that blood would not have accomplished its purpose and there would be a spirit running rampant in the earth forever.

Jesus did not allow any spirits the ability to run rampant. The final blood came gushing from his side and that was just the amount needed to conquer every spirit, every sin and every temptation. This is why the Bible declares that Jesus was tempted by all manner of temptation. He saw it all and conquered it just as a believer can through the power of his blood. Through me.

After three days, Jesus rose from the dead with all power in his hand. He had conquered the physical world. He still had one more task to accomplish. Jesus had yet to perform the same duty that the high priest did in the tabernacle of Moses. The high priest performed the duty in the physical world. Jesus now has to complete this duty in the spirit world. The book of Hebrews declares "But Christ came as High Priest of the good things to come, with the greater and more perfect tabernacle not made with hands, that is, not of this creation. Not with the blood of goats and calves, but with His own blood He entered the Most Holy Place once for all, having obtained eternal redemption." Once Jesus poured me out in the tabernacle, his work became complete.

The demise of Judas Iscariot

Judas Iscariot

> "Then one of the twelve, called Judas Iscariot went to the chief priests and said, 'What are you willing to give me if I deliver Him to you?' And they counted out to him thirty pieces of silver. So from that time he sought opportunity to betray Him."
> — Matthew 24:14-16

"I am Judas!"

I am one of the twelve disciples of Jesus and probably one of the more recognizable by name. Of course, Peter is known, as well as Matthew and John. I may not be as popular as they are but I am definitely more recognizable than Bartholomew, Thaddeus or Phillip. I was so close to Jesus that I became the treasurer and kept charge over our money. I loved Jesus and he loved me.

I didn't come to love Jesus for his money or his desire for money. He certainly didn't have much of either. My loyalty to Jesus came from an entirely different source.

When I met Jesus, he was not as popular as he grew to be. He had a handful of followers who began to walk everywhere with him. He asked me to follow him. I decided to because I was intrigued. I had never heard anyone speak with the authority in which he spoke. It was what he said and how he said it. He talked about

God as if he knew him. I had never heard anyone speak like that. Then he spoke to priests or soldiers or anyone as if he was not afraid. This confidence was one that none of us had ever seen.

This particular part of his personality is why I chose to follow him. I was always curious as to what he would say or do next.

This still does not explain my loyalty. I grew loyal to him when he began talking about restoring the kingdom. Our people have been under the thumb of the Romans for centuries. They abuse us, they tax us, and they turn our own against us. Any talk of revolution has been extinguished by authorities; but not Jesus. He spoke openly about establishing a new kingdom and I was so impressed that I was willing to do whatever it took to fight the establishment.

I've heard story after story of how we are the chosen people of God and how he sends a man to come and rescue his people. There are stories of Joseph and Joshua, and of course Moses. When God delivered his people through Moses, he destroyed the evil Pharaoh who had oppressed the people. God destroyed Pharaoh's army with one crushing blow. This is the kind of act we need now and Jesus seemed to be the man to do it! He has no fear.

Every time I thought Jesus was preparing us to make a military strike, he disappointed me. I remember when Jesus was questioned about paying taxes. I knew the answer that he would give would solidify our position against the evil oppression by Rome. By whose authority do they have to tax the

Jewish people? We are God's chosen and elect! They should pay taxes to us! They should bow down to our king! Caesar should pay the tax and our faces should be on the currency! If Jesus overthrows this regime, we can put his face on the money! This answer will mark a defining moment in our allegiance to Jesus. We have been following Jesus and given up so much. It's about time we receive something for our loyalty. Now is the time for our people. We are the new order. Jesus calmly asked for a denarius. He took it in his hand and looked at both sides. As he handed it back, he says "Render unto Caesar the things which are Caesar's, and unto God the things that are God's." No one said one word after Jesus makes this declaration. Those that questioned him are now silent for fear of the manner in which he answers questions. My friends are silent because most of the time we are trying to figure out the riddles that Jesus speaks in. I, however, am silent for a different reason. I'm so surprised by his answer that I do not know what further to say. Render unto Caesar?

    I then remember the one event that angered me the most about Jesus. We had just returned to Capernaum and a Roman soldier approached us. We didn't know what he wanted, nor why he was approaching. He walked directly to Jesus and removed his helmet. He almost bowed before Jesus and I saw the look in his eye. He had a look of desperation on his face. He begins to tell Jesus that his servant is sick unto death and almost pleads with Jesus to heal his servant. Jesus agrees! Why are we going to save a Roman's slave? The Roman then forbids Jesus and says that he isn't worthy of Jesus coming into his house! This man understands authority. He is both under authority of commanding officers and in charge of at least one hundred soldiers for he is a Centurion. He has the authority to tell any given soldier to go and that soldier goes as directed. He has the authority to request that any given soldier report to him and that soldier reports as directed.

Understanding authority, he considers himself not worthy to have a man with the authority that Jesus has to even enter his home. He instead asks Jesus to simply say a word and he believes his servant will be healed. Upon hearing this Jesus turns toward us and says that he has never met anyone with this type of faith! He says that he has not heard of anyone with this man's faith in all of Israel! Jesus then looks at us and says "Many Gentiles will come from all over the world, from east and west, and sit down with Abraham, Isaac, and Jacob at the feast in the Kingdom of Heaven. But many Israelites, those for whom the Kingdom was prepared, will be thrown into outer darkness, where there will be weeping and gnashing of teeth." I could not believe what I was hearing! Jesus said that these Gentile dogs would sit with father Abraham at a feast! I was disgusted by this claim, yet I held my tongue and said nothing.

There were so many instances where I felt let down by Jesus. Time after time, I felt it opportune that we take a stand and instead he spoke peacefully or in riddle fashion. So many times we collected money and instead of applying it to a strong revolt, we gave it away.

When I felt let down, this was not a feeling of

slight disappointment. Instead, my heart would drop. I felt that this revolution was something that we were owed. This was something that was due to us. This was supposed to happen. God sent us a messenger; a Savior. Yet, instead of saving us, he wants us to be friends with our enemies. He wants us to love those who oppress us. He wants us to turn the other cheek when someone slaps us in the face!

I had spent many days thinking of how different our lives would be if Jesus was king. I thought of John and Peter and James as members of the ruling class of the new government. I saw myself running the treasury of our new nation. Matthew would collect taxes from the underbelly Roman class. This was to be a new world order but instead, he wants to coexist as brothers. Brothers with the dog Gentiles! I was completely broken. This Jesus is not the savior and the hope of our people as I had been lead to believe. Instead, he is a sorcerer who speaks fables and lies.

After the incident with the question of taxes, I'd had enough. I had no money. I had given up my home and belongings. What does this life benefit me? I'm tired of hearing of a Kingdom that is not here while I have to bow to an evil oppressor. I can't do this anymore. I don't want to follow Jesus another day! I can't openly leave. What was I to go back to? I couldn't defy him in front of the others; they are all so loyal at this point that I will be stoned.

I know that the Pharisees would love an opportunity to arrest him. If they could arrest him and put him in prison then at least it would give the brothers time to come back to their senses and go back home. Peter may stay loyal and maybe John but the rest would leave him in a matter of days. We could get back to our various trades and get on with our lives.

Then there are others, like myself, who are still waiting for our true king. We need to regroup and plan the revolution. In order to accomplish this, we need this Jesus out of the way. He will lose popularity and we can make people forget him. I just need an opportunity to have him handed over to the counsel.

One day, we were at Simon the leper's home. Jesus had miraculously cured him of his leprosy. While there, we were eating and talking. Many had gathered around Jesus to hear him speak. This was a common occurrence. A woman approached him with an alabaster flask of perfume. She walked right up to him and broke the flash. She began to pour perfume all over Jesus' head. I could tell by the fragrance that it was very expensive perfume. This was so wasteful!

We could've taken this flask of perfume and sold it for a large sum of money. Some of us attempt to stop her and Jesus forbade us. He told us to let her continue because he won't be with us forever, but we will always have the poor. This proved to be my breaking point. I would stand for no more of this foolishness! The others can stay. I am not doing this any longer. First, he allows this wasteful spending of expensive perfume. Now he admits that he isn't a king who will restore Jerusalem. Instead, he says we will always have poor people among us! This was the statement that pushed me over the edge.

I knew that the Pharisees would listen to me. They

know that I am a follower of Jesus. I also know that they are willing to pay a hefty price for me to deliver Jesus to them. I can restore some of what I have lost in these last three years and regain my life back. Jesus will be put away and our lives can go back to normal as we await the real king.

My heart was pounding in my chest as I awaited a member of the council. I felt strongly about what I was about to set up, yet I have never been so nervous in my entire life. I wasn't told who I would be meeting with. Much to my surprise, not only did more than one member of the council show up to meet me but Caiaphas, the high priest, did as well. I had never met the high priest or other members of the ruling sect. He didn't say much yet he never took his eyes off me.

The transaction was swift. I agreed to deliver Jesus. They gave me a sack filled with silver coins. Thirty pieces of silver, to be exact. All I needed now was an opportunity.

When the Passover approached, the brothers and I prepared the feast. I had decided to not betray Jesus during the feast; for fear that some of his followers may revolt and oppose him being arrested. I'm sure most of his followers would oppose. I thought I had to be very strategic in planning his betrayal. The time and the place were crucial. I had no intent for it to happen when it happened.

As we were finishing the meal, many of us were talking amongst ourselves and Jesus makes a statement that silences the room. He simply says that one of us will betray him. Immediately, I lost my breath. I didn't say anything but my heart began racing. How could he have known? Or does he know of another with the same thoughts I have? I didn't say a word. First a slight murmur, then whispers. Then one at a time... "Is it I Lord?" "Lord will I betray you?" Jesus never looks at me or anyone else. He is staring straight ahead. His eyes are focused and his glance is unshaken.

    Within this brief moment, I realize how different I am from everyone else and I begin to lose my fear of Jesus knowing my intentions. Everyone is scared that it is them. They would each be devastated to find that they could possibly be the one who would let Jesus down. Each of the men is considering himself and what it would take to make them betray a man like Jesus; a man they love and follow. For the first time, I do not share in the heart sentiments of my brothers. I don't feel the same. I know it is I who has decided to turn Jesus in. I already know. My fear is not whether or not I could be the one to do it. My thoughts instead shift to whether or not Jesus will expose me as the man to betray him.

    Jesus then says, "It is one of you twelve who are eating from this bowl with me. For the Son of Man must die, as the scriptures declared long ago. But how terrible it will be for the one who betrays him. It would be far better for that man if he had never been born!" Jesus and I had just taken a piece of bread from the same bowl! I became so offended that he said that he wished I had never been born that I stood immediately! That was my breaking point and I decide to betray him that very night! My concerns about the

Passover feast were now gone. I decided to do it!

I started to storm out of the room, when he stopped me. This was the first time he looked at me. He looked at me eye to eye. In an instance, I remembered first meeting him and hearing him speak. I remembered him challenging authority and how impressive of a man he can be. He speaks just as authoritative to me and says "What you go to do, do it quickly." Fine teacher! I will!

I knew he would pray in the garden after the meal, so I led the chief priests and guards there. I told them to follow my lead and that I would greet Jesus with a kiss. Once I did, they were free to arrest him. When we approached the garden, I saw Jesus from afar, speaking with a few of the brothers. Peter, James and John were with him. I walked directly to Jesus and kissed him on the cheek. "Rabbi!"

One of the guards pushed me aside and grabbed Jesus by the arm. A commotion ensues immediately and a fight breaks out. The chaos erupts so fast, I could barely make out what was happening. I saw James running away. Peter and I locked glances with one another. The guards began to beat Jesus with their fists. They were kicking him as they pulled him along. I don't know why they were beating him. They were only supposed to arrest him.

I turned and ran as fast as I could. I didn't look back but I heard the commotion of the scuffle. I ran and hid. I didn't want the other brothers to see me. James and John saw me. Peter clearly saw me. Jesus looked me in my eyes. This was not how it was supposed to happen. They were supposed to arrest him; not beat him.

That night I tried to rest, but could not sleep. I sat alone until the sun rose. I felt nauseous and didn't want to move. I had to find out what was to happen to Jesus. How long would he be in prison? I have never felt such guilt. I know that what I did had to be done. The others will come to understand at some point. We have given up everything! We have no homes to go back to! Jesus was a charismatic sorcerer who could charm people into believing almost anything, yet his promises are unfulfilled! I had to do it...so why did I feel so bad right afterward?

I was curious as to what they would decide about Jesus, yet I could not muster the courage to go find out. I spent the entire day alone. I could not eat or sleep. My thoughts raced in hundreds of directions as the hours passed. In one instance, I felt justified in my actions. In another moment, I felt incredible shame and guilt. In the next second, I knew I made the right decision. Three seconds later, I could not believe what I had done. I thought of the brothers and which ones I felt I could talk to. Who would support what I had done? Which would try to kill me? I thought of his mother. I thought of some of the people in whose homes we had eaten. He has touched so many lives, yet let so many of us down. I had to do it! Yet, was it the right thing to do? It was the right thing to do! I think. In one moment I began to laugh uncontrollably as I remember the way that I felt when he accused me of my impending betrayal. In another instance I wept bitterly recognizing the fact that he had become a friend and I turned him in. Did I do the right thing? Of course I did! Did I do the right thing? No! How could I have?

I thought that everyone would understand if Jesus was simply gone for a season. If the counsel sentenced him to three years in jail, his following would go back to their normal lives and we could then await our true king. No one would remember what I had done and no one would speak on it. We could rejoin our prior occupations and move on with our lives. This is what I wanted to happen.

On the morning of the second day, I could no longer wait. I had to find out where they were keeping him and what they had decided. I covered my head as to not be recognized and made my way from my hiding place. As I began to see people, I felt like all eyes were on me. It seemed as if every private conversation between two or more people was about me. I felt as if everyone was glaring in my direction and pointing at me. Had the word gone out that I betrayed Jesus and am the reason he had been arrested?

I saw a man walking alone and made my way toward him. I had to find out what happened to Jesus and what his sentence was going to be. When I asked him what the fate of Jesus was, his answer rendered me shocked and speechless. "The prophet from Nazarene is condemned to death. He will be crucified." What? Crucified? They are going to kill him?

I couldn't believe it! I truly couldn't believe it! This was not the agreement that I thought I was making! I didn't think they would kill him! I raced to the synagogue. At this point, I didn't care who saw me. Being recognized in town was the least of my concerns. I arrived in a heap of sweat and out of breath. I approached the leading priests and elders and declared that I had sinned. I told them that I had betrayed an innocent man! "What do we care? That's your problem," they replied dismissively. My heart dropped in my chest. I felt like the wind had been knocked out of me. My head began to hurt immediately and I became filled with both anger and remorse. I took the money bag filled with the silver coins that they had given me and I threw it at them. For this level of disrespect to a chief priest, I could have been imprisoned. I did not care. What I had done was far worse than any prison cell. I betrayed a man who does not deserve to die. Jesus was not guilty of any crime worthy of crucifixion but these men are going to put him to death…and it was all my fault!

    As I ran out of the temple, my heart was pounding in my chest. I didn't know where I was running to; I just ran. My thoughts became the times where Jesus spoke to children. He always smiled and showed them compassion. I remember when he spoke to an open tomb and commanded the dead man Lazarus to come out. Lazarus walked out as if he had never died! I remember when Jesus taught a huge crowd of people and was able to feed them all with just a few fish and loaves. I remember him walking on water toward us and I remember him calming the raging sea. These thoughts now raced through my head, one after another after another after another, causing my head to hurt. What have I done? This man was not guilty of any crime worthy of death! Yet he is now sentenced to die! What have I done?

The brothers are going to hate me! They are going to want me dead! They may stone me! Peter is going to kill me if he can find me! Both James and John loved him! They are going to be devastated, as will the others! This is my fault! This is all...my...fault! I am no longer worthy to live! I can't go on! I have crucified an innocent man!

Through my tears, I secure one end of the rope around the tree. The other, I place around my head. It rests on my shoulders, around my neck. I tighten it to my neck where I cannot breathe fully.

"Jesus!...I am so sorry!...I didn't know they were going to kill you!...I didn't know they were going to crucify you!...You did nothing that deserves death!...I am sorry Jesus!...I...am...so...sor...r...y...I...aaaaaam...aaaaaaam....aaaaa...mmmmm..... mmmmmmmm...... mmmmmmm.....sssssssssss...ssooooorrrr..."

Christ is captured

The Roman Soldier

"Then the soldiers of the governor took Jesus into the Praetorium and gathered the whole garrison around Him."
— Matthew 27:27

"I am a Roman soldier!"

I pledge allegiance to Caesar. We are the world's largest military force. No one rivals the Roman Empire; no one ever will. No one dare come against our force. We are the Romans!

The Jews are beneath us. They are somewhat of a primitive people who need structure and guidance. They only respond favorably through harsh discipline and a set structure of government. We allow their silly religious customs,but we control them. We don't want to destroy them, for they are important to us for taxes and merchandise. Therefore, we allow the religious ceremonies and traditions as not to cause them to revolt or riot. We allow them to manage their own commerce, goods, and services. We allow them the freedom to raise their families in the traditions of their forefathers. Yet, they bow to Caesar. They show allegiance to Rome as the controlling nation. Most will bow their head if even I walk by.

The rights of the Romans will always overpower the rights we afford the Jews. In court, a Jew will never win against a son of Rome. We have the right to imprison any person we deem a threat to Rome, Caesar, or our way of life. Prison sentences can last a lifetime if we see fit. We arrest, we discipline, we imprison. This is the manner in which we rule this society.

My company was given orders to arrest one of their criminals. This man was saying that He is the son of God. Apparently this is against a Jewish law. I am not as familiar with their laws and customs but this has outraged many of the Pharisee ruling class. They brought the matter to Pontius Pilate who sent it back to Herod. Herod sent this man back to Pilate and Pilate has condemned him to be beaten and crucified.

The scourging was brutal. All disciplinary action is severe, but this case was indeed barbaric. My company members gave him 49 lashes with the whip which is also called the cat of nine tails. This particular whip has nine leather lashes, each with a piece of bone, metal or glass in its tip. This whip would cause death to most men. By the time the scourging ended, there was blood everywhere. His body had been torn to pieces. He was still alive which seemed to be miraculous. The real miracle was that he never fought back.

I have seen criminals run, cry, scream and beg for mercy. I have seen men of large physical stature reduced to the demeanor of a child at the sting of the tip of the whip. I have seen the beating cause many men to lose consciousness. Yet this Jesus character never did any of those things. He never cursed us or his tormentors. He never tried to run or even escape. When being led to the whipping post, he calmly walked and allowed the guards to secure him. I have never seen anything like this display.

One of the soldiers fastened thorns to Jesus' head to mock him. He shaped it into a circular crown shape. When he pressed it into Jesus' head, he began to bleed even more. He looked as if he would pass out but he didn't. He still refused to resist or fight back. Blood began to pour across his face from his forehead. Blood was pouring down the back of his neck. Blood was pouring down the sides of his face and onto his shoulders. I could not believe he had the strength to pick up the large wooden beam but he did. He picked it up with whatever strength he had left and began to walk the hill to his place of death.

As I walked through the crowd, many of the Jews were crying. Many were simply looking on. Some were shaking their fists. We had to clear the path for him and the other criminals, but Jesus kept falling. He seemed to be under tremendous pressure trying to maintain the weight of the wood. Beyond the whipping, the beating, the punching and kicking; beyond the thorns and the blood, it was a very humid day. He was being tortured. The thought crossed my mind a few times to the extent of his crime. Was all of this punishment worthy of him just saying he was the son of God?

By the time Jesus made it to the top of the hill, he had to have someone help him carry the wood. He makes it and we began to nail him to the cross. Large spikes were driven through his hands and feet. I was surprised he had any blood left in him but both his hands and feet began to bleed immediately and profusely. The cross was lifted high into the air and he hung between two other criminals. He was in bitter agony, but still never complained.

Some of us took his clothes and divided them. We cast lots for them as a joke. I took a piece of his clothes and stuck it into my belt, as to not lose it.

As the afternoon wore on, I kept looking up at him. He hung there dying; still bleeding. He would say a few words but he never answered his harsh critics who yelled at him to come down and save himself. He even spoke to one of the other criminals. By this point he looked exhausted, yet he still remained alive.

The heat of the day had subsided some. The cross he hung on was drenched in his blood. It seemed that the entire crowd that had followed this spectacle all day was still watching. Not a single individual has decided to leave. As difficult as it may seem to look at a bloodied man, it was equally difficult to turn away. As a soldier of Rome and a facilitator of the discipline that I am ordered to perform, this by far has been the most gruesome of penalties for seemingly the smallest of offenses.

Suddenly, the sky began to darken. It was such an instant change as one second it was bright and sunny and in a moment, it darkened. Jesus lifted his head and stared at the sky. He screamed into the air asking why he had been forsaken. This caused a stir in the crowd of Jewish onlookers. Some began to yell at him once again. The sky grew even darker. He says a few more words and then his head drops. When it does, I knew he had died. I can tell as his body began to go limp and the weight of his adult frame began to pull at the hands being held only by iron spikes. He has died.

    The ground begins to shake violently and the sound of thunder cracks the otherwise silent sky. This was by far the loudest roll of thunder I'd ever heard. Everyone begins to glance at one another nervously. Could this possibly be a result of Jesus dying? The instant his head drops, the ground shook! I didn't know what was going on!

    The shaking of the ground worsened and the Jews and some of the soldiers began to run for their lives. The other two criminals were still alive. One of the soldiers yelled out to break their legs so they would die faster. One soldier runs to the criminal hanging closest to him and slams his legs with a huge club. The criminal begins screaming from the pain. His body immediately drops as his legs can no longer support him on his cross. The other criminal begins screaming before he is even hit. He anticipates the impact and screams even louder when his legs are simultaneously broken. His body drops limp under his weight as well. They will both be dead of suffocation soon.

    Jesus however, is already dead and I have taken a few steps toward him hanging on the cross in the middle. The crowd is now in a chaotic fury as they run away to protect themselves from the earthquake, thunder and lightning. I see another soldier pierce his side with a spear, instead of breaking his legs since he has already died. I look at his mother who is weeping. I look at a man consoling his mother who must have been one of his close followers. I look at a few others who have chosen to stay amidst the running soldiers

Conversations of the Crucifixion

and Jews. I then look up at him. His body is covered in blood and bruised. His head is hanging down. His hands and feet have holes in them.

This man never fought back. This man never cursed me, the other soldiers or his accusers. He asked his God to forgive us all instead. Jesus never ran from this penalty. He seemed to calmly accept it. Now that he has died, the earth is shaking and the sky has turned to the dark of night. Truly this man was the son of God!

I am a Roman soldier. I am a citizen of Rome by birth. I am not familiar with any god other than the gods of the Greeks. Yet this man Jesus, who hangs before me... the God of the Hebrews... he has changed my opinion. He has changed my life. This God is the true God. He is real and this man that we have killed today was indeed his son!

Peter

> *"And I also say to you that you are Peter, and on this rock I will build My church, and the gates of Hades shall not prevail against it."*
> *– Matthew 16:18*

"I am Peter!"

I am one of the twelve disciples of Jesus. I walked with him when he began his ministry. When I met Jesus, the first thing he said to me was; "Follow me." I left my family and my job to do just that; I followed him.

For three years, I tried to learn all that he had to teach us and show us through his actions. Most of the time, I admittedly got it wrong. I often spoke out of turn and more times than that, spoke out of context. When I thought I was saying the right thing, I was completely wrong.

One of the earliest and most memorable times between Jesus and I was when he began to call me Peter. My original name is Simon, but Jesus gave me the name Peter which means "The Stone." In the Greek language, there are two different words to denote a stone. Petros is the masculine form of the word and Petra is the feminine. Petros means a detached stone. This is a stone that can be broken off or taken away. Petras means a mass of rock. This is a boulder which cannot be moved. I didn't realize how important this new name and these definitions would mean to me until years later.

    I first met Jesus while my brother and I were fishing with our father. There was something about him that drew people. Just to hear him speak or see him relate to children was incredible. I've never met anyone like him so I immediately followed him. Soon after, I began seeing him perform miracles. It was amazing! I was utterly amazed when I saw him feed so many people with that little boy's fish and loaves. I began to think that he really could be God's son.

    I've heard the old stories about the Messiah. I know that tradition says that God would send a king for His people, just like He did when we were in Egypt. God sent Moses to speak to Pharaoh and bring God's people out of bondage. We are all familiar with that story. I don't know how many of us believe it actually will happen again. For those who do believe, most don't believe Jesus is the one. He doesn't come from royalty. He isn't a member of the ruling class. He isn't of the tribe of the priests. At the same time, I witnessed him do things I have never seen any man do. There was a part of me that found it unbelievable, yet a part of me wanted to believe.

    Right after he fed the crowd of people, he told us to get into a boat and go over the Sea of Galilee to Capernaum. My brother Andrew and I are from Capernaum, as is Matthew. We were all excited to see our families until the storm hit the sea. We had rowed four miles and the boat was being tossed. It was at that moment when we saw him. We thought it was a ghost; I certainly did. Some screamed of fear. Some were so afraid that they were silent. I heard his voice as he called out to us. He told us not to be afraid and that it was him. It was Jesus, walking toward us on top of the sea!

Jesus was walking on water! It was unbelievable! Walking on water is impossible! No man can walk on water! There was a part of me that found it unbelievable, yet a part of me wanted to believe.

I immediately asked Jesus if I could walk out to him on the water and he told me to come. Without hesitation, I stepped out of the boat and began to walk toward him. There was a part of me that believed! Before I knew it, I had almost reached him walking on water, but no man can walk on water! No one has ever done this! This is impossible! I looked down at the waves crashing against my legs and I felt the wind pushing me in my back. What was I doing? There was a part of me that found this unbelievable and I began to sink. I cried out for Jesus to save me and he grabbed my hand. He pulled me up and told me that I had little faith. I felt empowered and dejected at the same time for there was a part of me that believed and did it, yet there was a part of me that doubted and failed.

Then there was the time when Jesus called James, John and I alone. We walked to the top of a mountain and immediately there was a bright light around him. It was so bright that I fell on my back. I couldn't look directly into the light. I noticed that James and John were on the ground as well. I covered my eyes with my arm and tried to look through. The light was blinding but I heard Jesus talking. I could only see his feet but there were two other men standing with him. I squinted my eyes to see who it possibly could be. It couldn't have been James or John because they were lying on the ground with me. It couldn't have been any of the others because they could not have gotten to the mountain top so quickly. I was astonished when I recognized the two men. It was Moses and Elijah and they were talking to Jesus! Of course I've never met Moses or Elijah but I knew it was them! It was totally unbelievable! How is Jesus talking to the patriarchs of old who have already died? No man can speak with the dead! Yet this was Jesus! Maybe he actually is the son of God. Although a part of me found this to be unbelievable, a part of me wanted to believe. I yelled out "Jesus! It is a good thing that we are here! Allow us to build three altars for you, Moses and Elijah!" Then a voice came from above saying "This is my Son in whom I am well pleased." I closed my eyes for a split second and when they reopened, Moses was gone, Elijah was gone, and the light was gone. Jesus stood alone. I looked around and only Jesus, James, John and I remained. I didn't know what to say or do. Jesus simply smiled and gestured for us to follow him down the mountain. Why did I say what I said? I felt empowered to have experienced this, yet dejected for yelling out. We slowly made our way down the mountain, no one uttering a word. I was curious to what James and John thought of my outburst but dared not ask. I thought that my outburst was what led to the patriarchs disappearing as they had. I couldn't believe that in a moment of such a miraculous vision, I blurted out what I did.

   Then, there were some of the little things that I experienced with Jesus. When we prepared the

Passover meal to celebrate, Jesus began to wash everyone's feet. I couldn't believe this! Why was God's son stooping down to wash our feet? This was unbelievable! This was the Messiah and the King! He deserves to have his feet washed, not to wash the feet of others... of men... of sinners! Since I didn't think it was Jesus' place to wash our feet, I refused to let him wash mine. Jesus then told me that if he could not wash my feet, then I had no place with him. I had to believe that he came to serve and not to be served and the truest test of leadership is one who will serve. I thought that I was saying the right thing but I was wrong once again.

Then came the life changing moment for me. This conversation with Jesus changed my life forever. He asked us who men said that he was. We have heard him called a prophet. We have even heard him called Elijah. He then asked us who we said that he was. I spoke up loudly "You are the Christ! The son of the living God!" I knew who he was, because I had seen and heard so much. I saw him do unbelievable things. I heard him preach unbelievable messages. A part of me wanted to believe that he is the son of God; a part of me didn't. I knew because I felt something. When I heard the question, I felt a peaceful comfortable feeling and it resonated throughout my very being. I know that he is. I can feel it. I can hear it somehow. I know who Jesus is. Jesus answered me and said "Blessed are you Simon, for flesh and blood has not revealed this to you but my Father who is in heaven. You are Peter and upon this rock I will build my church." I've never felt so honored. I've never been so envied by the others. I felt overjoyed and empowered.

My heart was full. Immediately afterward, Jesus began to tell us that he was going to be arrested, tried and crucified. He said that he would be betrayed and led away by sinners. I couldn't believe what he was saying! Never! I would never allow Jesus to be taken! He is God's son! I would not allow it! I spoke to Jesus with haste and told him that I would not allow this! Jesus rebuked me swiftly by saying, "Get behind me satan! You do not understand the things of God!" Jesus had just called me blessed! He had just said that I was the Stone! He said that he would build his church upon me! Now he is speaking to satan in me! The others looked at me; no longer with envy or jealousy but with disdain. Jesus yelled at satan in me. The joy I had in my heart moments before had been replaced with feelings of hurt, guilt and confusion. I then tried to tell Jesus that if he must die, then I would die with him. He smiled and told me that before the cock crows the next morning, I would deny him three times. I'd never felt so empowered and dejected in my life.

That night, Jesus once again called James, John and I, and led us to the Garden of Gethsemane. He instructed us to pray while he went alone to pray. As he walked away into the distance, I began to pray to God. I wasn't sure what to pray for or what to say. I found myself not saying much and growing very tired. We had just eaten the Passover meal and were all quite tired. I began to feel comfortable and must've fallen asleep. Jesus woke each of us up and told us to pray again. He was shaking and noticeable disturbed. I have never seen Jesus with a look of uncertainty. He has always been very sure of himself, even when speaking to the ruling class or Romans. Yet now, he looks scared and extremely worried. I glanced at James and John who were speechless. I began to pray but this time, I prayed for Jesus. I was afraid that he was afraid. I asked God to protect him and heal him from whatever troubled him. Although my intentions were probably noble, I once again ran out of words. How does one pray to God about his own son? I didn't know what to say. I laid there motionless, growing more tired than before. I felt a hand on my shoulder shaking me. It was Jesus. His face was wet from sweat like he had been baptized in the Jordan. He asked why we couldn't stay awake to pray for even an hour. I then heard footsteps and saw torches approaching. We had been followed and I looked around to see soldiers. I heard chains in their hands. Some carried clubs and swords. Some carried fire lit torches. I saw some of the priests and I saw Judas. Judas! He had led them right to us! He was turning Jesus in! I could have killed him! What was he doing! When he kissed Jesus on the cheek, the guards went to grab him. I immediately drew my sword and struck a soldier and sliced off his ear! I was protecting Jesus! I was protecting God's son! I just prayed to God to protect him and now I am doing that! I know that this is the right thing to do! Jesus however rebukes me! He tells me to put my sword away and that if I live by the sword, then I will die by the sword. He placed his hand on the wounded soldier's ear and heals him. I was so confused that I ran. I thought I was doing the right thing and I was wrong once again. I ran.

    I run and hide until they carry him away in chains. They beat him, arrested him and dragged him away. I followed closely but didn't want to be arrested as well. When the soldiers dragged him into the inner court of the priest's chambers I waited outside. I couldn't believe what was happening but I didn't say anything. I tried my best to see through the crowd while hiding in the midst of them.

    A young girl approached me. She was a doorkeeper. I could tell by her age and attire. Many of the nobility have slave girls as doorkeepers. Most of them will not speak unless they are spoken to. This girl however boldly approached me. She stated that I was a follower of Jesus. She began to tell the people standing around that I was one of the followers. Some of the men began to look at me. Two of the guards stopped walking to see what the commotion was about. I looked around quickly and said that I didn't know Jesus. I turned quickly and moved away from the girl and the direction where the guards were.

    I moved away from the court entrance and instead moved toward the gateway. The further I move away from the direction of the crowd, the better. When I reached the gate however, another young woman said something to me. This time she was with an older man. They both said they had seen me with Jesus and the others. I will never forget her accusation as long as I live. "You were with him! I've seen you with Jesus! You're one of his friends!" Maybe she saw me with him during our time in Jerusalem. She may have been in the crowd when he taught on the Mount of Olives. She could have possibly been waving palms when we entered this city just a few days ago. It is very clear that she saw me with Jesus and with her accusation, the crowd begins to mumble. My response was swift and confident. "I swear by the great name Jehovah that I do not know the man!"

Before I was able to move away, another man implicates me. Then another. Then a third. I then recognized one of the high priest's servants. He was making his way through the crowd toward me to see about the commotion. There were a half dozen men pointing at me and saying that I knew Jesus and was with him. By the time the servant reached me, he had even more men to accuse me. He pointed directly into my face and hurled his accusation. "Did I not see you in the garden with him?" I emphatically declared that it wasn't me. I have never been so afraid in my life. These men wanted to kill me. They wanted to put me on trial like they were going to do to Jesus. He further accuses; "Surely you also are one of them, for your speech betrays you!" With this, someone tries to grab me and I see soldiers making their way through toward me. I yell directly back at him and those around him. "Damned! Shut your mouth! All of you! I do not know the man! I swear I do not know the man!"

Seemingly, as if the final word from my mouth initiated the cock's response, I heard the crow. My thoughts reverted back to the words of Jesus. "Before the cock crows, you will deny me three times." Of the many things I've heard Jesus say over the years that I was with him, no statement has ever weighed so heavy on my heart than this one. I've heard him say that he loves me. I have heard him talk of his love for the will of his Father. I have heard him say things about the unseen God that I have never heard anyone else say. I have never heard anyone speak to the authority of the Pharisees and priests the way that he had. Yet none of these words remotely compare to his now accurate claim that I would deny him three times. I had given up everything. I had risked everything. I put all of my trust and faith in Jesus. Now that it matters most, I let him down. I allowed my fear of being beaten and arrested to completely consume me. Jesus knew I would fall short. He knew I would fail him. He knew I would say the wrong thing as I have done in the past. I broke from the crowd and ran. This time I wasn't running from the guards. I was running because that was all I had left. I was running from Jesus. I was running from myself. I was weeping terribly and I ran until I could run no more. I collapsed and wept until I had no more tears. I wailed and cried out. I wanted to die.

I felt as if I was the worst of his friends. I am much worse than Judas. Judas betrayed him, but I denied him. James, Matthew, and Bartholomew argued to sit next to him, but I denied him. Martha grew angry with Jesus for taking so long to see Lazarus, but I denied him. The Pharisees called him Beelzebub, but I denied him. A group of lepers were healed by Jesus and didn't bother to return to thank him, but I denied him. The synagogue leader chastised Jesus for healing a woman on the Sabbath, but I denied him. The guards in the garden beat him and cursed him, but I denied him. Of all the people who did brutal and malicious things to him, I am now the worst. I denied him, just as he said I would. Of all the times I've felt dejected in my life, I've never felt as low, dejected, lonely and as much of a failure as I did when I denied Jesus three times.

"Blessed are you Simon, for flesh and blood has not

revealed this to you but my Father who is in heaven."

Over the next three days, I didn't eat. I did sleep, but not much. What consumed me were the words that Jesus spoke to me during the years that I've known him. "Blessed are you Simon, for flesh and blood has not revealed this to you but my Father who is in heaven." This life changing statement is now in my mind like never before. As a result of what happened, I began to pray to Jehovah God. Unlike times before, I knew what to say. I knew what to utter. I began to tell him how wretched I was and I asked that he would consume me. He never did. I began to then weep for Jesus and I prayed for him. I thought I would never see Jesus again. I began to pray for my brothers; all of them. I had not seen any of them since the arrest. I even prayed for Judas, and as I did, I remembered what Jesus taught us; "Forgive us our trespasses as we forgive those who trespass against us." I then asked to be forgiven. Jesus told me many times of the love of God and of his many attributes. Maybe He would look upon a terrible person, as I was, and forgive me. Maybe He would strengthen me in my time of need. Although I have done the most terrible thing, I asked for true forgiveness. Through my tears, I felt it. I recognized the feeling from when Jesus posed the question to all of us; "Who do you say that I am?" As I answered him then, I felt something that caused me to know that he is God's son. I knew it with a certainty then and once again, I know with a certainty now. A part of me has always wanted to believe, yet a part of me has always had doubt. It was through my tears and prayers however that I fully believe my statement of who he is. I felt his friendship in the midst of my tears.

I remember the warmth I felt it as he taught, and I felt that at my lowest point. Just when I thought he would discard me was when he picked me up.

At that moment, I understood his statement. The most powerful statement he ever said to me. The statement that changed my life forever. "You are Peter and upon this rock I will build my church." The way that Jesus spoke, it had suddenly become clear. He said "you are Petros." This was the movable stone. I had been movable. One minute I would believe. The next minute I would doubt. One minute I would be bold and courageous. The next minute I would feel fear. One minute I was ready to step out of the boat. The next minute I felt myself sinking. I was the movable stone. He then said that upon this Petra, he would build his church. This was the unmovable rock. There were times where I got it right. I said that he was the son of God. I said that I could walk on water as he did. What was revealed to me was not by flesh and blood but by the Spirit of God. This revelation is unmovable. There were times where I was solid in my conviction. Other times I was acting on pure emotion and adrenaline. At times I was right, at times I was wrong. At times I believed, at times I doubted. At times I was Simon, at times I was Peter. There were times where he called me Simon. There were other times where he called me Peter. There were even times where he called me Simon Peter. Upon this revelation, Jesus was to build the church. The church is built and sustained by people just like me. I did a terrible thing, but I am still a part of the church, because Jehovah God restored me. I got it wrong most of the time, but Jehovah God forgave me. I was weak and incomplete at times but Jehovah God fulfilled me. I didn't understand the teachings all the time, but Jehovah God has empowered me. The church is a body of people like me. There are times when we are Simon and there are times when we are Peter. There are times where we act out of emotion. There are times where we are led by the Spirit of God. Jesus built the church on a man who has flaws but was forgiven and made whole. Although I felt a great sorrow that the priests had killed Jesus, I gained comfort in knowing that I was forgiven by God.

On the first day of the week, I was with John when we saw a woman running toward us. She was weeping and almost out of breath as she quickly approached. It was Mary Magdalene. She was almost hysterical and I begged her to calm down. I wasn't sure what had happened. I knew that tensions were high and that many of us were in fear of the Jews and were hiding from them. Maybe someone else had been arrested. Maybe it was the mother or brothers of Jesus. Mary could barely get her words out yet she uttered "They have taken the Lord out of the tomb, and we do not know where they have laid him." I couldn't believe what she was saying! Someone had taken the body! Immediately we ran to the tomb. I ran as fast as I could, but John outran me. When he arrived at the tomb, he looked inside, but I passed him and fully entered. I saw the linen garments that Jesus was wrapped in. I also saw the linen cloth that was on Jesus' head and it was folded by itself apart from the other garments. I saw the grave clothes but there was no body. Jesus' body was gone. Someone had rolled away the stone and taken him. Mary was right. Jesus was not there.

This is the worst thing that could have happened! Jesus has been crucified and now his body has been stolen. This is why the brothers have been hiding. We know that many of the Jews want to kill us also because of the teachings of Jesus and how we followed him. Now they have come and entered the tomb and taken his body away.

That evening, we assembled in the upper room where the Passover was celebrated. We locked ourselves in, for some of us feared the Jews and what they might do if we were discovered. Everyone was there except Thomas and Judas. John and I told the others what we saw at the tomb. Everyone was in a state of shock and no one knew what we ought to do. Suddenly He appeared in our midst. He didn't come through the door. He simply, but amazingly, showed up! Some of us thought it was a ghost, but Jesus raised his hands and said "Peace be with you!" He showed us his hands and his side where he was pierced. I became overjoyed! Jesus was crucified and now stands amongst us speaking with us! Jesus then gives us an instruction that I will never forget, "As the Father has sent me, I am sending you." He then breathed on all of us and said, "Receive the Holy Spirit. If you forgive anyone's sins, their sins are forgiven; if you do not forgive them, they are not forgiven." When He breathed on me, I felt the same energy that I felt when I stepped out of the boat. I felt the same feeling as when I told him that he was the Son of God. I felt empowered and I have never turned back from that feeling on that evening.

I saw Jesus two more times after that night and each time he further confirmed my newly strengthened belief system. Jesus has changed my life more than I ever could have imagined. I will never forget him. When we spoke, he gave me final instructions to feed his lambs and to feed his sheep. The last words that Jesus spoke to me are the same two words that he first spoke to me; "Follow me." I indeed have followed him.

I am following him right now as I stand with my fellow countrymen. These men have traveled to Jerusalem to celebrate the Passover. Men have come from lands near and far. They have asked if we have been drinking since they heard us leave the upper room. When my brothers and I left the room this morning, we were all filled with the Spirit. It caused us to speak in other tongues and every man visiting Jerusalem heard their native language spoken by us. They were confused. They wanted to know if we were drunk. I stand in the midst of them with the full confidence of my friend Jesus… the Messiah.

"Listen carefully, all of you, fellow Jews and residents of Jerusalem! Make no mistake about this. These people are not drunk, as some of you are assuming. Nine o'clock in the morning is much too early for that. No, what you see was predicted long ago by the prophet Joel."

"In the last days, God says, I will pour out my Spirit upon all people. Your sons and daughters will prophesy. Your young men will see visions, and your old men will dream dreams. In those days I will pour out my Spirit even on my servants—men and women alike—and they will prophesy. And I will cause wonders in the heavens above and signs on the earth below—blood and fire and clouds of smoke. The sun will become dark, and the moon will turn blood red before that great and glorious day of the Lord arrives. But everyone who calls on the name of the Lord will be saved."

"People of Israel, listen! God publicly endorsed Jesus the Nazarene by doing powerful miracles, wonders, and signs through him, as you well know. But God knew what would happen, and his prearranged plan was carried out when Jesus was betrayed. With the help of lawless Gentiles, you nailed him to a cross and killed him. But God released him from the horrors of death and raised him back to life, for death could not keep him in its grip. King David said this about him."

"I see that the Lord is always with me. I will not be shaken, for he is right beside me. No wonder my heart is glad, and my tongue shouts his praises! My body rests in hope. For you will not leave my soul among the dead or allow your Holy One to rot in the grave. You have shown me the way of life, and you will fill me with the joy of your presence."

"Dear brothers, think about this! You can be sure that the patriarch David wasn't referring to himself, for he died and was buried, and his tomb is still here among us. But he was a prophet, and he knew God had promised with an oath that one of David's own descendants would sit on his throne. David was looking into the future and speaking of the Messiah's resurrection. He was saying that God would not leave him among the dead or allow his body to rot in the grave."

"God raised Jesus from the dead, and we are all witnesses of this. Now he is exalted to the place of highest honor in heaven, at God's right hand. And the Father, as he had promised, gave him the Holy Spirit to pour out upon us, just as you see and hear today. For David himself never ascended into heaven, yet he said, 'The Lord said to my Lord, Sit in the place of honor at my right hand until I humble your enemies, making them a footstool under your feet.'"

"So let everyone in Israel know for certain that God has made this Jesus, whom you crucified, to be both Lord and Messiah!"

Every man is attentive to my every word! I can feel the Spirit of God and the same energy and boldness that I felt when I stepped out of the boat! I feel empowered! I feel confident! A man stands and asks, "What must we do?"

"Each of you must repent of your sins and turn to God, and be baptized in the name of Jesus Christ for the forgiveness of your sins. Then you will receive the gift of the Holy Spirit. This promise is to you, and to your children, and even to the Gentiles, all who have been called by the Lord our God."

I finish speaking and men begin to approach my brothers and me, to receive baptism and to join us. Thousands upon thousands of people come. I see my brother Andrew praying with a group of men. I see Bartholomew doing the same. Thomas is telling others of his witness to Jesus. All of my brothers are boldly confessing Jesus and what he taught us to do. I think back to the lessons I've learned over the last three years and I remember what Jesus said to me; "You are Peter and upon this rock I will build my church." I've never felt so empowered. I've never felt so bold. I've never felt so confident. I am Peter! Upon the revelation that Jesus is truly God's son, the church will stand forever.

Pontius Pilate

"And Pilate asked him, Art thou the King of the Jews? And he answering said unto them, Thou sayest it."
— Mark 15:2

"I am Pontius Pilate!"

I am the fifth Prefect of the Roman province of Judaea. As prefect, I serve under Emperor Tiberius. I am a judge. I deliver the sentence. I am the final decision maker. I grant a man his freedom or his sentence. I have the power of life or death over a man. I deliver this power and authority on a daily basis. Many men have been sentenced to die by the hands of our soldiers; merely because of the way my gavel has fallen. Life and death are in the swing of my gavel and the power of my will.

I walk into litigation with the authority to overrule the magistrate. The power of my office affords me this right and authority. The final verdict rests squarely on my shoulders.

The Sanhedrin Elders have asked me to judge and condemn one of their outlaws. This man Jesus has made false claims of being a king and God's son. I have no matter with these accusations as this is the Jewish culture and doctrine. The Jews do not hold the authority to condemn a man to death as my office does so they have brought this matter to my court. Often times, I make deals with the leaders of their religious sect to best benefit my office. Not knowing the particular instances in this case, I will have to see how this situation may benefit.

They bring the criminal to me for me to question him. As I look at this man, he is common looking. Most criminals glare at me and I am often pleased that they are in chains. Jesus simply stands before me. He doesn't glare or curse my office. He simply stands before me. The Pharisees are clinching their jaws as they glare at him. Some shake their fists as they hurl accusations at him. Everyone is yelling at once and I can feel the hatred focused toward Jesus. They hate this man for the claims he has made. If they had their way, they would kill him themselves. I lift my hands to quiet them. I want to question Jesus.

"You are Jesus. There has been much said about you. The Jews, your own people, seem to be quite upset by the claims you have made. What say you in regard to these claims?"

Jesus does not answer. He simply stares back at me. He has a still presence. He almost looks sad, yet he stands confident.

"Are you the king of the Jews?"

"It is, as you have said." This answer by Jesus throws the Pharisees into a riotous fit.

"What further proof do we need? You heard it direct from him!"

I quiet them again. I am intrigued by this man. He does not offer a defense or state that these claims are not true. He simply stands in my presence looking back at me. How can a man so calm be a hated criminal? What affair have these Jews brought me into? I face the Jewish leaders.

I find no basis for a charge against this man.

The Pharisees insisted, "He stirs up the people all over Judea by his teaching! He started in Galilee and has come all the way here!"

Galilee? I turn back toward Jesus. "You are from Galilee?"

If Jesus is from Galilee, then I can send him to Herod! Galilee is Herod's jurisdiction. He can be tried there and I can be through with this matter. Herod is in Jerusalem at this time. Surely he can handle this case and I can stay out of this affair.

I rule that this matter be tried by Herod Antipas. If this man Jesus is from Galilee, then it is only right that he be seen there and tried.

The Jewish leaders don't seem happy at my verdict, but I quickly exit the room. I will hear nothing more on this matter. I have more important items to tend to and I look forward to a restful evening from the events of today and this trial of Jesus who has so aggravated the Jews.

A restful night is exactly what was necessary for me. I feel rejuvenated and relaxed, especially after the day I had yesterday with the Pharisees and the man from Galilee. As I enter my courtroom however, I am confronted by the same Jewish leaders as yesterday, and the man they have accused; Jesus. Why are they back? Why is Jesus still bound? I sent him to Herod yesterday!

"We need you to condemn this trouble maker! Herod has returned Jesus to your court for sentencing!"

What! Herod sent him back to me? Why?

The Sanhedrin council responds all at once. I raise my hand to silence them and point to one of them to speak. "Herod questioned Jesus and he never spoke back. He never answered any of the questions asked of him. He stood quietly. You have to make a decision today! He needs to be condemned!"

"Gather in the Praetorium! I will render my decision there!"

The guards drag Jesus away in a hurry and the Jews follow closely behind yelling and shaking their fists. I take a deep breath and whisper to myself to calm myself down. I then walk to the Praetorium and take my place on the judgment seat. A crowd of Jews has formed in the courtyard unlike any I have ever seen. It seems all of Judea has gathered to hear this verdict. This man Jesus has either enraged or enraptured thousands of Jews.

"I have examined Jesus before you and find no fault in this man touching those things whereof you have accused him! Nor does Herod, for he sent him back to us and behold, nothing worthy of death has been done by him!"

Immediately there is uproar in the crowd. There are so many people shouting that I cannot hear a thing they are saying. I raise my hands to silence the crowd but this time it doesn't work as well as when I had a small number of the Sanhedrin in my court. I have to signal the soldiers to take position. It is only after the soldiers begin to move that the crowd quiets down.

"What has this man done that is worthy of condemnation?"

My question causes all the more uproar. The people are shaking their fists and some are yelling accusations. The soldiers begin to move closer to the crowd and I keep them back by raising my hand again. I am in total disbelief of the outrage this man Jesus has caused. I glance toward him and he calmly stands, not offering a word in his own defense.

In the corner of my eye, I see a messenger of my wife approaching. The young woman is moving quickly toward me. She rushes past Jesus and my personal guards. She is allowed to approach as she is recognized as my wife's messenger. She leans in close to my chair and whispers into my ear. "Your honor, an urgent message from your wife, 'Have nothing to do with that innocent man, because in a dream last night, I suffered much on account of him.' She persuaded me greatly to deliver these words to you." I nod my head and motion for her to depart. She quickly moves away. I look back at Jesus who is now looking at me yet turns to face the crowd again. What am I to do? My wife has sent word to me to not condemn this man; yet if I don't, I fear an uprising.

I stand and approach Jesus. He turns his head to face me.

"Don't you hear these accusations against you? Have you nothing to say in your own defense?"

Jesus says nothing.

"Don't you understand that I hold the power of life or death over you? I can sentence you to live or die by the decision I make today!"

My question seems to awaken Jesus from his silent slumber. He responds, "You do not have authority over me. Only my Father in heaven has such authority."

We stare at each other speechless for what feels like an eternity. I don't want to say or do what I am about to say and do, but Jesus is leaving me no choice. I turn away from him and walk back to my seat, yet I don't sit down. I raise my hands again to quiet the crowd.

"I will punish this man for the accusations he has made against your law! Then we shall bring him back to see what you will have of him!"

There is yet another roar from the crowd as the guards pull at the chains that are around Jesus' neck. I order the captain to scourge him and bring him back to me. Seemingly before I can say another word, Jesus is hauled off to the whipping post.

I look for the messenger that delivered the message

from my wife. I want to confirm what my wife has said but the messenger is gone. I walk toward a soldier who is standing post.

"I want you to send an executive order through your chain of command to order more guards. Whatever decision is made for this Jesus fellow may cause a riot amongst his people and followers. We would be wise to be prepared for any outbursts or outrage."

"Yes sir!" The guard hurries away.

I want to spend a few moments alone. I want to think. I want to try and reason this case in my mind. I sit alone and close my eyes. I rub my forehead and lay my head back against the back of my chair. There is no evidence to condemn this man. If he has offended the Jewish religious leaders then that is their problem. What has that to do with my court or the Greeks?

"Sir... the prisoner has been returned."

The minutes must have flown by and maybe I daydreamed. Nonetheless, the guards have brought Jesus back. It seems in my mind that he just left moments ago, but apparently a significant amount of time has passed and the guards have punished Jesus. Hopefully this will satisfy the Sanhedrin and we can put this case to rest.

Yet as I approach the Praetorium, I look at Jesus standing there. He can barely stand. He is dressed in the robe that Herod gave him to mock him as king, yet it is now drenched in blood. He has blood all over the body parts not covered by the robe. I can see on his hands that are shackled together that he is bleeding profusely. They almost killed him! They must've have beaten him within an inch of his life!

I look at the crowd. Most seem as shocked as I am as they see him standing there. He is still quiet. He is not fighting back. He is not defending himself. He is simply standing there.

I face the crowd and they immediately start to murmur. The murmuring turns quickly into a small roar. One man in the crowd yells "Crucify him!" This turns the crowd into frenzy. I look at the captain of the guard and he motions to his men to take their position in case of a riot. I raise my hands to speak to the crowd.

"Has this man not suffered enough? What am I to do with this man of yours?"

One of the Pharisees yells, "He is no man of ours! Away with him!" But what has he done? "Crucify him!"

Each time the declaration to crucify him goes forth, the crowd screams, mostly in favor. I span the crowd looking for someone to support Jesus and I don't see many.

I raise my hands again to silence the crowd. It takes longer to silence the crowd this time. If it were not for the soldiers, I fear a riot will break out.

"As custom during this time of year, I will release a prisoner to you! I will summon one of the criminals in the prison and you can decide which criminal will be set free!"

　　I turn to the captain of the guard and speak to him directly. "Have your men send up Barabbas!" There is no way this crowd will choose to free him over this Jesus character!

　　I turn toward the crowd again and one of the chief priests quiets the crowd himself. He then speaks directly to me. "This fellow claims to be a king! This is a direct insult to Roman rule and to the Roman deification of Caesar! There is no king over us other than Caesar!" This creates a huge response amongst the crowd. The people are now yelling louder than they had before. Guards begin to move in to maintain order. I sit on the throne in a state of unbelief. I still cannot grasp the deep hatred for this man, simply because he claims to be the son of their God. The soldiers have kept the riot from spilling out and becoming too difficult to manage.

　　Three guards have come up with Barabbas in chains. He is accused of being an insurrectionist against the Roman Empire. Unlike Jesus, Barabbas is pulling away and struggling with the guards. It takes all three guards to bring him to the platform opposite Jesus. He squints once the sunlight hits his face and he glares at the huge crowd that has gathered. He looks toward me and then at Jesus. Upon seeing Jesus, Barabbas stops struggling. I think he is taken aback by the brutal scourging that Jesus has undergone. Jesus' face is busted and bruised. His face is beaten so badly that his eyes are almost closed, his cheeks are swollen. There is a good amount of blood coming from his mouth. Barabbas seems to be in disbelief as I am.

"I have brought you Barabbas! According to the custom, I will release one prisoner to you today! Who will it be? Jesus or Barabbas?"

This question has caused the largest response by the crowd! It seems as if everyone is yelling for Barabbas to be set free! Guards are struggling to keep order as this crowd is voting for Barabbas.

"What am I to do with Jesus your king?" The response is to crucify Jesus! Everyone in the crowd seems to want Jesus crucified! What has he done worthy of crucifixion?" The response is even louder to crucify him!

I turn to the captain of the guard and instruct him to fetch a bowl of water. He gives the command. I try to reason with this crowd again. "What is this man guilty of?" I point to Jesus. "What has he done?" The only response is to crucify him.

When the water arrives, I place my hands into the bowl. I begin to wash my hands.

"I am washing my hands of this matter! I am not responsible for the blood of this innocent man!"

Someone screams at the top of their lungs "Let his blood be on our heads!" Then let it be as you have said!

Immediately Jesus' chains are yanked, pulling him backward. Simultaneously, Barabbas is released. He still seems to be unaware of what just took place.

I motion for the chief priests to approach, and they do. I speak directly to them and declare that I am ordering a sign posted above Jesus' head that reads Jesus of Nazareth, The King of the Jews. They immediately protest and begin to state that Jesus is not their king and that he falsely claimed to be so. I simply say to them, what I have written, I have written. So be it.

These men have caused the death of an innocent man, and have tried to use me as their vessel to do so! These Jews have made a mockery of my office and this court. Yet above those reasons, I looked into the eyes of Jesus. Jesus is no criminal. He is no prisoner. He is not an insurrectionist and poses no threat to Caesar or Rome. He is led away like a lamb going to slaughter, simply for claiming to be the Son of God. If his claim is true, then may mercy fall upon me and all who witnessed this event. May God have mercy on us all.

The trial of Jesus Christ

The Whipping Post

> "Then they will hand him over to the Romans to be mocked, flogged with a whip, and crucified."
> — Matthew 20:19

"I am the Whipping Post!"

I secure the man who is to be tortured by the whip. I am an unmovable stump, secured into the ground. No matter how hard a man tries to escape, once he is handcuffed to me, he stays in place. There is no escaping your fate once fastened to me.

Criminals know what their fate is, as soon as they see me. They are carried and dragged by the Roman guards, screaming and fighting. I strike fear in their hearts because I hold them in place for their beating. I don't care how much they scream or pull. I don't care how much they try to release their wrists from the shackles. There is no escaping me.

Every man who is chained to me leaves a piece of himself upon me. Some have left pieces of their flesh. Some have dug their fingernails so deeply into me that pieces of the nail have become embedded. They all leave blood. The Bible declares that the life of the flesh is in the blood. Every man that leaves blood leaves a piece of himself; a piece of his life with me. There have been so many men fastened to me that over time, I have forgotten their names and their faces but not their stories. All I have is the life story that they stain me with.

The crimson stains that now color me represent each man's story. Some are whipped for robberies. Some are whipped for unpaid taxes to Rome. I can point to a particular stain and tell you that man's struggle. I am a myriad of stories and a kaleidoscope of stains of blood. I will hold on to these stories for I am forever stained with the life blood of these men.

When they brought Jesus to me, he walked and did not fight back. He wasn't struggling with the soldiers. He wasn't being dragged. He walked calmly and allowed his wrists to be shackled. They tore his clothes off of him without a fight. He stood patiently and waited to be hit. The next few moments would forever change the way I remember this man, Jesus. Although he looked like any other criminal who has been chained to me, he treated the experience very differently. I had never seen anything remotely close to what I was about to witness.

Instead of screaming at his loudest, he was whispering. I listened carefully until I was able to make out what he was uttering. "My Father, it is my ultimate pleasure to perform your perfect will. It was our good pleasure to slay the lamb before the foundation of the world. Before there was ever sin in the earth, this purpose was established. It is now the appointed time and I accept the penalty for man so they won't have to. Father, forgive these men and keep my heart pure." I've never heard any prayer like this. It sounded sincere and heartfelt.

As soon as he uttered the last word of his prayer, the first blow struck him across the back. It's at this point where most criminals curse loudly, as they feel the sting of the first blow. Jesus never cursed. As the blows continue and the intensity increases, Jesus holds on and keeps his composure as best he can. He never curses or swears. He never speaks directly to the soldiers or the onlookers. He continues to pray.

They beat him from the standing position, to a kneeling position, and finally to a lying position. They whipped him mercilessly on his back, his legs, his arms, his head, his stomach, and his face. Never before have I seen a man beaten so brutally and not die. Jesus remained alive the entire time, never ceasing his prayer. His prayer never changed. It was always giving thanks. It was full of praise to God. It was continually asking for forgiveness for the men who were torturing him. How can a man ask God to forgive the very men who are abusing him so badly?

It wasn't until I took the stain that I began to see his story and understand his thought process. His blood tells a story, the likes of which I had never heard. He was able to forgive the Romans who tortured him because he taught to forgive not just seven times, but seventy times seven. He taught that the heavenly Father will not forgive unless you forgive your neighbor. Jesus taught his disciples how to pray by declaring, "Forgive us our trespasses as we forgive those who trespass against us." Jesus lived this declaration even as he was being tortured.

His blood tells a story of the redemption of men and women. To be redeemed is to be rescued by paying a price. Jesus is willing to pay with his life to rescue lost men and women. The price is his life for the life of the flesh is in the blood.

His blood doesn't tell a story of robbery, murder or tax evasion. His blood doesn't tell a story of revolution against the Roman Empire. Instead, his blood tells a story of prayer. Jesus prayed so earnestly in the Garden of Gethsemane that he sweated profusely from the anxiousness of his prayer. Jesus often went alone by himself to pray only to return stronger and prepared to heal and deliver. Prayer is man's way to communicate to God and Jesus taught his disciples how to pray.

As Jesus' blood joins the blood of other men that were fastened to me, His will forever be remembered and have an undying impression on me. He was different. He, I will never forget. He showed an exemplary position of prayer and forgiveness that I had never seen. He truly lived what he believed, and practiced what he taught. In the face of excruciating pain, torment, and unbearable circumstances, he prayed to forgive.

The Whip

> "So Pilate released Barabbas to them. He ordered Jesus flogged with a lead-tipped whip, then turned him over to the Roman soldiers to be crucified."
> — Matthew 27:26

"I am the Whip!"

I am also called a cat of nine tails. I have nine leather ends and each end holds a piece of metal or bone. I am a viscous instrument. When I attach to something, the metal pieces attach and rip it apart. I can tear skin off the back of any man. For this reason, men fear me. Men respect me. Men tremble when they see me. No man wants to face me.

I have grown a hatred for men. Every man I come across, I make it a point to try to injure. If I hit a man, he will be injured. If I barely touch a man, he can be injured. If a man picks me up the wrong way, I can injure his hand. I swing purposely with the intent of injuring men. One man carried me as he walked along. I purposely swung to hit his leg and I injured him. One man swung me too far back and I injured his head. The flesh of men is nothing more than meat to be torn from the bone and I am just the instrument to do that.

The Roman soldiers brought me out that day and

I saw the next victim. They tied him to the whipping post and tore off his clothes. The first time they swung me at him; I grabbed his back and pulled. Nine pieces of metal cut into his skin. Nine pieces of metal caused him to bleed. I hit his back and ripped his flesh off. Blood flew off his back in every direction.

The first time I hit him, I tried to kill him. The first time I hit him, I tried to rip his back off. When I hit him, I tried to break him. I hated this man because I hate all men. The second time I hit him, I tried to injure him beyond healing. Every time I hit him, I wanted to kill him.

The soldiers swung me with all their might, but that didn't matter. It wasn't by their might, but my might ripping Jesus. Not their power, but mine. The more I whipped him, the more he bled. The more I tore at him, the more his flesh would fly in the air and land on the ground or on the soldiers. With every swing I grew more intent on hurting him, injuring him, and killing him.

They turned him over, and I began to whip his stomach. I ripped his stomach. I ripped his chest. I ripped his arms. I ripped his neck. I ripped his shoulders. I ripped his face.

Other men were whipped unconscious, but not Jesus. He was very awake and very aware of his pain. Whenever I whip a man, I hear him pray. I hear him beg for mercy. Jesus didn't pray that way though. He would not ask for mercy like all other men. Jesus would not beg me to stop like other men begged of me. Every man asks God to take his life and to end the pain. If the man would simply die, the pain would stop. I cause every man to pray. I can hear them scream the prayers. This happens every time I am applied. They cry, they scream, they beg, they pray. This is the pattern of every man. This pattern never changes. All men are alike and I hate them all.

When the soldiers finally stopped whipping Jesus, when I finished ripping him apart, I heard him pray. His prayer was different than any prayer I had ever heard. He didn't ask God to take his life. He didn't ask God to kill the soldiers like other men do. Instead, I heard him thank God. I heard him ask God to forgive the soldiers. I heard him thank God for the opportunity to save mankind. I heard him worship God.

The very men that I hate so much, he was praying for. The men who were using me on him mercilessly, he was praying for. He has the opposite feeling that I have toward men. I have grown to hate all men; he was beaten because he loves all men.

I see now that Jesus endured the pain of the whip for a greater purpose. By taking on the pain that I inflict, he also takes away the pain of sin. Sin has delivered a pain far worse than I could ever put on a man. Jesus faced me so men can be delivered from the pain that sin brings.

Men fear me. Men respect me. However now, I respect Jesus. I respect Jesus because I know that no man could endure what I just did to him unless that man had a greater purpose. For Jesus, the greater purpose is love. His love is so great that he took the pain of me tearing the skin off his body to accomplish a task. His love is so great that despite the agonizing torture that I put him through, he would still face me to fulfill his purpose. He had to take the pain that I bring forth to take away the pain of mankind.

The Crown of Thorns

"And they clothed him with purple, and platted a crown of thorns, and put it about his head."
— Mark 15:17

"I am the Crown of Thorns!"

On the day that Jesus was to be crucified, I was on the side when they led him in. As the soldiers dragged him by, I turned away as to not look at him. I didn't want to look at him, yet I couldn't stop looking at him. Although I wanted to see him, I didn't want to see him. He had been brutally beaten and he was a spectacle to look at.

Furthermore, I was too busy to take the time to look at him. I was busy doing my job and I had to get back to work. My job is to protect beauty. I protect the rose. The rose is the most beautiful flower that God has ever created. When a man wants to show a woman the full extent of his love, he gives her a rose. No flower on Earth is as beautiful as a rose. My job is to make sure that the rose is protected.

No rose has ever grown without me protecting it. Every rose has a stem. Every stem has thorns. Every thorn has a dangerous point. I grow in every direction throughout the entire length of the stem. My job is to protect the rose. This is my job, and I perform my job well.

You must be careful when handling a rose for when you do, you handle me. If you handle me incorrectly, I can bring pain. I'm designed to cause men to bleed. I'm designed to cause pain. I'm designed to protect.

I protect the rose because of the extreme beauty and its delicate nature. As a rose is beautiful, it is equally fragile. A rose's petals can fall off almost effortlessly. The petals are soft, fragile, and moved by the slightest cause. Too strong a wind can dislodge the petal of a rose. God designed me to protect what is most delicate to Him... I am the watchman of God's beauty. This is my job and for centuries, I have performed well.

The Roman soldiers were leading Jesus right past me when they suddenly stopped. They look at me. They think about me. They think about how much pain I can bring if I'm touched. They want to mock and ridicule Jesus. They know that some of his followers call him king. Just a few days ago, there was a large gathering and thousands of people chanted "Hosanna to our king", as he came into town. The people had crowned him king.

Jesus being called a king meant nothing to me. It probably meant nothing to the Roman soldiers, other than them having a reason to laugh at him. It did however disturb the Rabbi and his court of priests. They realized if Jesus was called a king, it may present a threat to the Romans. Caesar is in authority and Herod is king. If the masses of Jews promote this Jesus as their king, a threat is presented to the Romans. The Romans will retaliate, enforce harsh penalties, tighten their political grip, and remove the priests from their authority in the temple. Caiphas, the high priest was the most upset upon learning that Jesus was referred to as king.

Since the soldiers are mocking Jesus, they decide to insult him by designing a crown for him to wear. They knew that the Jews called him a king and that every king deserves a crown. The soldiers carefully take me and shape me into the form of a crown. They begin pressing me into Jesus' head. As they press harder, blood begins to pour from his scalp…and the sides of his head… and the back of his head. Each of my points drives through his skin and his scalp. Each of my points drives through his temples and forehead. I feel his hair, his head, and his skull. The deeper they press, the more he bleeds, until blood pours from each part of his head.

I become covered in his blood as he is bleeding all over me and then it happens! I'm pressed so deep into the head of Jesus that I see his mind. I see his thoughts. By seeing his thoughts, I begin to understand my purpose with him today! I see him reminisce the past in which I was created. I was created in the Garden of Eden. In Genesis, the book of beginnings, it states in chapter 3 that I grew from the ground as a result of man's sin. When man fell, I grew. When sin entered, I grew. When man disobeyed, I grew. I grew as a result of sin. I grew as a result of man's falling away. I grew as a result of mankind losing his connection with God.

I am a result of sin! Just as I am painful to touch and to bear, so is sin. Just as I bring agony and grief, so does sin. Just as I can damage and rip, so can sin.

I begin to see how God dealt with sin in the Garden. He covered Adam and Eve's sin with the blood of an animal. The animal was sacrificed to cover the sin of man. The animal's fur covered Adam and Eve and the animal's blood covered their sin.

Now I understand! The only way to cover the sin of man is with his blood! Jesus is bleeding all over me, and the blood is covering the sin. The blood is wiping away the sin. The blood is cleansing the thorns!

I see my purpose now! I can see what he is thinking! I can see what God is thinking! He is thinking about you! To the woman who feels exhausted because she is raising children on her own, he is thinking about you! To the brother who feels guilty because of the same temptation over and over, he is thinking about you! To the married couple who see no hope in their future, he is thinking about you! To the young person struggling with their sexuality, he is thinking about you! To the person who feels lost and down and out, he is thinking about you! To the person who struggles with an illness that has kept them down for many years, he is thinking about you! To the person who has lost it all due to heavy financial burdens, he is thinking about you! To the person who is called to minister, yet fear is gripping their heart, he is thinking about you! To the woman who feels guilt from deciding to abort a pregnancy, he is thinking about you! To the man who's lost his family, he is thinking about you!

I see his thoughts and I see my purpose. I recognize why God created me. I am to protect what is most precious to God. I am to protect you! You are beautiful to God. You are the most beautiful creation God has ever made. You are precious in His sight and I am to protect that beauty. You are also fragile. Many of you are tossed to and from with every wind of doctrine. My purpose is to protect what is most precious to God. I am to protect His children.

By Jesus bleeding all over me, he is covering me with his blood, just as the blood in the Garden covered sin. Without his blood, all over me, you would be uncovered. Without his blood pouring over me, you would be lost. Without his blood consuming sin, you would be disconnected and without hope.

Because he is bleeding on me, you are covered. Because he wears me as a crown, he carries the weight of sin, so you don't have to. Because the innocent one is bleeding, the guilty one is covered. Because he is taking the pain for you, you don't have to take it.

My purpose is to protect what is most precious to God. God's children are as beautiful, yet as fragile as a rose petal. Therefore, Jesus wore me; the result of sin as a crown, so His children won't have to. I am the ultimate sacrificial protection.

Christ bearing his cross

Simon of Cyrene

"Now as they came out, they found a man of Cyrene, Simon by name. Him they compelled to bear His cross."
— Matthew 27:32

"I am Simon!"

I had traveled to Jerusalem from Cyrene in order to celebrate the Passover. This was a trip that every Jew wants to make at least once in their lifetime. For those of us living in Cyrene, it is more difficult a task to attend as our city is 900 miles from Jerusalem.

The journey takes a month's time and is not an easy journey. There are arduous weather conditions, encounters with wild animals, desert marauders, and a host of other obstacles that can hinder the progress of those attempting to attend. Nevertheless, I completed the long trip and arrived in the city before the Feast had begun.

Passover is one of the most important celebrations of the year. We remember how the God of our forefathers passed over the homes of the Hebrews who had the blood of the lamb on the door posts. He passed over those homes and did not allow the plague to come upon them. Instead, the plague of death hit the firstborn of all the Egyptians who did not cover their homes with the blood. The Law states that we are to observe this phenomenon forever. We are to take a lamb from among the flocks with no bruises, no broken bones or blemishes. We are to slaughter the lamb for the Feast and pour out the blood as an offering to the God of our forefathers. This is a special time of year.

Even with the height of the largest and most important festival of the year at hand, I had no idea the commotion and uproar that was taking place in Jerusalem when I approached. I had never seen a crowd like the one I encountered as I entered the city. There seemed to be thousands of people huddled around a path winding through Jerusalem. I could barely see what the commotion was about. Some were screaming and shaking their fists, many were weeping uncontrollably. There were also a great number of Roman soldiers which confused me. The Romans do not celebrate or recognize the customs and feasts of the Jews. Why had so many soldiers come to attend dressed in full battle armor?

I asked the first person I came into contact with what the roaring of the crowd was about. He yelled that the prophet from Nazareth was being beaten and crucified! He told me that this Jesus was tried and will be killed for proclaiming to be the son of God and the King of the Jews. He was thought by some to be the foretold Messiah. For this, he was being killed.

I was shocked! Jesus is being crucified? The word of this man Jesus had traveled far and wide. Even I had heard of him. The most interesting story that I'd heard about him was that he raised a dead man named Lazarus and brought him back to life. I had obviously never met Jesus; I had never even seen him. Upon learning of the day's events, I began to press my way through the crowd to get a glimpse of the man who said he was the son of God.

I pressed my way past men, women and children. Some of the women were shielding the faces of the young children so they would not see the man. The women wept bitterly. Some of the men cried too. Some hurled curses and accusations. I still could not see the center of the attention; the man named Jesus. Once I got to the front line of the crowd closest to the pathway, I encountered a line of soldiers keeping the crowd back. They were lined one next to the other, while a few were actually on the path with the man. I still could not get a good look at him. The soldiers on the path were encircled around him. It looked as if they were kicking and punching him.

By the time I could see clearly, he was almost in front of me. He was on all fours and blood covered his face. I couldn't see what he looked like. It looked like he had thorns stuck in his head and there was blood pouring out from under the cloak he was wearing. One of the soldiers kicked him in the side and yelled for him to continue on. Jesus fell to the ground and was kicked several more times. Two more soldiers yelled for him to get up. It looked as if he was dying right there on the road. He was barely moving. I could see that he was trying to push himself up. The beam of wood that he had been carrying on his back had fallen beside him. The man could barely stand. How do they expect him to carry the wood?

I didn't notice one of the soldiers staring at me. The Romans lorded their authority over the Jews every opportunity they could. You did not want to be singled out by a soldier, nor stared at. I assume this is how our forefathers felt when they were under the thumb of the oppressive Egyptians. I'm sure you would not want to be singled out by an Egyptian taskmaster. I had been so focused on seeing the face of Jesus that I didn't notice the soldier walk toward me and push me in my chest. I stumbled back into the people behind me. He ordered me to pick up the wooden cross that Jesus had been carrying.

    I stood motionless. I didn't want to help this man. I didn't know him. I had never met him. I have no allegiance to him. If I pick up the bloody piece of wood, I will be desecrated according to the Law and not able to celebrate Passover! The soldier shoved me into the path and ordered me again. This time, the other soldiers saw me and joined him in ordering me to pick up the cross. Suddenly, the situation came to the forefront of my mind. If I refused, I could be arrested for not obeying Roman authority. I could be tortured and sent to prison. I would miss the Passover. If I obliged, I would wear the blood of this man and not be allowed to sit at the Passover Feast. The noise from the screaming crowd quieted to a whisper in my mind. All I could hear at this point were soldiers who were once yelling at Jesus, now yelling at me. I looked at the cross beam on the path. I looked at Jesus who had made it to his feet somehow. I could now see his face. His face was beaten badly. His eyes and face were swollen. His beard had pieces missing as if it had been pulled out. The thorns were coming out of his forehead like thoughts. He was breathing heavy and weary as if he was ready to fall. Our eyes locked in on one another and I saw something unusual. He wasn't sad or depressed. His eyes looked confident. I could tell he was in tremendous pain and anguish but he didn't look worried. Who is this unusual man Jesus?

I walked toward the wood and picked it up. Immediately I had the blood of this man on my hands. I situated it on my back and stood behind him. He stumbled forward and began to walk toward the hill on which he would be crucified. As amazing as it was that this man was still alive, I found it more amazing that people were still yelling curses at him. I could see men dressed as if they were the ruling class of Pharisees. Some of them watched silently but others were yelling and shaking their fists. The soldiers kept pushing him until he fell under the weight of their fists. Once on the ground, they began to pummel him with punches and kicks. He rolled around on the ground, yet never screamed out against his attackers.

I dropped the cross and went to help him up. I grabbed his right arm and tried to drape it over my neck and shoulders. I helped him to his feet. I now had the blood of this man on my face and body.

Once he maintained his footing, I picked up the wood and began to follow him again. We managed to make it to the hill. He stumbled his way up the hill where there were soldiers waiting to place the beams together and into the ground. When we made it to the top of the hill, He collapsed onto the ground and I fell under the weight of the wood. Three of the soldiers took the wood from my back and I slowly stood to my feet. I looked at Jesus as they began tearing his cloak and undergarments from him. I turned and looked at the women sobbing furiously into their hands. I glanced at the Pharisees who did nothing but watch and smile. I looked at the entire crowd of seemingly thousands who had gathered to witness this extreme torture first hand. I then looked back at Jesus.

I've never felt so many emotions flow through me at the same time. I felt sorry for him; a level of compassion I'd never felt. I felt angry at those who would condemn any man to die in such fashion. What crime is worth this permanent punishment? I felt disgusted that I was now unclean by the Law of our forefathers. I felt curious as to what this man really was about. Was this attention worthy of a claim to be the Son of God? I felt sick to my stomach watching the soldiers laughing at a fallen brother. They began casting lots for his clothing as if this entire event was a spectacle. I felt the pain of the weight of the wood that he had been carrying. I wanted to run crying, screaming, and pounding my chest at the same time!

I wanted to say something to him. I wanted to encourage him but that didn't make sense. He was hours from death! What encouragement was necessary or appropriate? I wanted him to know that I was on his side somehow. No words came as I backed away. I only had thoughts which came so rapidly that I could barely understand them. The same crowd that I had to push through to get to see him now backed away from me as I walked backward away from the three dying men.

The last image I remember was his cross being raised into the air. He had been nailed in order to secure him. I could no longer watch. I felt like a participant by the intrigue I felt. I turned and walked away yet the images of this day were grafted into my mind.

I couldn't sleep that night or several nights afterward. I tossed and turned with thoughts of Jesus' crucifixion. Seeing him crawling on the road was an image I will never forget. The emotional turmoil that I went through will not leave my heart for some time. I left that day with a strong desire to talk about him. I started by telling my family members and friends about the experience I had carrying his cross. I then began to share my story with my countrymen. I found myself talking to strangers next and telling them this most unusual story. I no longer felt disgusted about celebrating the Passover. I felt like I did a nobler feat by helping Jesus. Oddly, I am proud that I was selected that day.

It became widely known that three days after Jesus was crucified, He rose from the dead just as Lazarus was raised by him. Truly, he was the Son of God! This word went forth to many lands and crowds of people followed him after his death.

It still wasn't until years later that my experience reached its full potential in my heart and mind. A follower of Jesus; a tax collector, wrote a saying in a gospel portrayal of his time spent with Jesus. He wrote the words of Jesus where Jesus told his disciples, "If anyone desires to come after Me, let him deny himself, and take up his cross, and follow Me." I am the first person to actually adhere to these words! Upon reading this declaration by Jesus, I felt honored! I felt chosen! I feel as if I am indeed a disciple of His and I have picked up my cross and truly followed him! I thank the God of our forefathers for the opportunity to be the first to live out these words!

Christ dies on the cross

The Cross

> *"And he bearing his cross went forth into a place called the place of a skull, which is called in the Hebrew Golgotha."*
> — John 19:17

"I am the Cross!"

I am the most recognizable piece of the Crucifixion. I am the executioner! I am the symbol of death. When criminals are condemned to die, they crucify them on a cross. When men are worthy of death, they crucify them on a cross. I am the last resort. I am the cross!

I am worse than prison. I am much worse than stoning. When I bring death, I don't bring it swiftly. When a man is crucified on me, he hangs all day and all of his shame is exposed. I bring pain. I bring embarrassment. Most importantly, I bring death slowly.

The spirit of death is a companion. I'm so skilled at what I do that I have become the only inanimate object that death has chosen to work with. If a man faces a spear, he may see death but it isn't certain. If a man faces a club or sword, there is a chance he sees death. Death may or may not show his face. When a man faces me however, there is no question. It is with full certainty that death will come. Death and I have a working friendship. For this reason, I am finality.

Every man fears me. Men are humbled by me. The strongest of men are broken by me. I am unbreakable, yet I break men. I am unmovable, yet I move men's emotions. Some men weep bitterly as I hold them. Some move into a state of hysteria. Men have lost their original language and spoken in delusion when hanging on me. Men are reduced to a shell of the human state.

Some would call my attitude arrogance. I rather call myself confident. I am confident in the fact that I can take human life. I am confident in knowing the power I possess over the frail human mind and body. It was believed that men have breakable bodies but unbreakable spirits. I have proven that theory wrong for it is not long before the spirit of a man hanging on me is torn to shreds. I know the power I possess and how good I am at what I do. I am the cross; the friend of fear and the companion of death.

A man's final hours and last breath will be spent hanging on me. I will hear his last mutterings. I will hear his last whisper. I will feel when his heart ceases beating. I will know the exact moment when his blood stops moving through his body. I will know if the man goes into shock or dies of suffocation. I will feel his every movement. I feel his final flinch. I hear him cry, I hear him scream. I hear him beg for mercy. However, there is no turning back. I am the last resort.

When the soldiers select me for this particular day, they place me on the back of the crazy man from Nazareth. Some called him a king but others called him crazy. Some called him blessed, others called him blasphemer. Some called him anointed, others called him annoying. Some called him a lamb, others called him a liar. I see him and call him another criminal. When you've seen one criminal, you've seen them all.

There aren't too many crimes that result in death on a cross. I've hung murderers. I've hung criminals who have committed treason. I've hung men who have led revolts against the Romans. When I saw the man who would carry me, I knew of his crime for he declared that he was God's son. This goes against Jewish law and didn't seem worthy of a crucifixion. It doesn't seem as if the punishment fits the crime. Yet none of this matters. My task is to hang the man until he dies. That is what I will do. I'm overly confident that he will die upon me.

When they place me on the back of Jesus however, there is something different about him. When he picks me up, he's already bleeding. He had been brutally scourged and his body was ripped. His back is open and his arms are crimson red. There is blood everywhere. Blood is pouring from his head and blood is running down his neck. Blood runs heavily down his back. His legs had been beaten so bad that they're covered in blood. When he picks me up, his blood gets all over me. When they place me on his back, I feel the blood before I feel him. There's so much blood all over him that it begins to cover me. When his blood touches me, I feel a power. When his blood starts to drip on me, I feel a connection. I have never felt anything like this before!

I then realize what the connection is. The connection stems from our representation. Jesus represents divinity! I represent humanity! The Bible says in the first chapter of the book of Psalms that a man's delight is in the law of the Lord and in that law he shall meditate day and night and he will be like a tree. In Genesis 7, Noah puts the humans who are to survive inside of an ark made of gopher wood. Wood carried surviving humanity to safety through the flood. In the book of Exodus, chapter 25, Moses is instructed to build an ark of the covenant for the presence of God to reside. It is to be made of shittim wood and overlaid with gold. This represents royalty stretched out over humanity. In chapter 30, Moses is instructed to make the anointing oil with five ingredients. One of the ingredients is cassia wood. This represents the outer shell of a tree which must be stripped away to get to the inner sap. Just as man's flesh must be stripped to get to his spirit, so is the same in the wood of a tree. Wood represents humanity.

    I now understand the power that I feel. Divinity carrying humanity with his blood connecting us! This man is carrying the weight of humanity up a steep hill. The weight of man is so heavy that Jesus falls three times trying to carry me. He presses forward however, for his destiny is to die for humanity. When we make it to the hill, they lay him on me. They use nails to fasten him to me. Once he is secured to me, they lift me up. They raise me up to hold him but they lift him up to embarrass him. They raise me up to kill him, but they lift him up to shame him. They raise me up to crucify him; they lift him up to be crucified. Divinity stretched out over humanity with the blood connecting us!

    I hold Jesus high for the rest of the day. Through the heat of high noon, I hold Jesus high. He hangs while people in the crowd mock him. I hold him while some in the crowd cry for him. He hangs while soldiers tear his clothes and cast lots for his garments. He is high in the air as the priests mock him and dare him to come down. I hear one criminal mock him while the other asks him for help. I see his mother at my base crying for him. I've never seen such an outpouring of emotions for a common criminal. I've never seen so large a crowd gathered for a crucifixion. This Jesus of Nazareth is not a common criminal. He isn't a murderer. He isn't a thief. He never insights a crowd to revolt or riot yet so many have gathered to see him hang on me.

Then it happens. He drops his head and dies, and the ground begins to shake. Some in the crowd begin to run, fall and trip over one another. I continue to hold him up as the earth quakes. The people that were mocking him are now running for safety. A few that were insulting him are now running for their lives. Everyone seems to now realize who this man is. This Jesus who they have just crucified is indeed the Son of God! Jesus has changed the way that I see him! I once saw him as a common criminal, now I see him as the savior of humanity. I don't see him the same way, now that I know who he is! Now that I know who he is, he isn't the same and neither am I!

No one sees Jesus the same now that they know who he is. In addition, no one sees me the same, now that they know who he is! Instead of me being seen as a symbol of death, for the first time I become a symbol of life. People begin to see me as the greatest symbol of sacrifice in history. People begin to talk about me.

People write songs about me. People erect crosses in their churches. People wear crosses as jewelry around their necks. People get crosses tattooed on their skin. People send crosses on greeting cards. People make crosses out of palm leaves. I have become the symbol of all of Jesus' followers.

He has changed me! Jesus has changed me! I held the man who cares so much that he changed the way the world sees me. I held the man who cares so much that he changed the way that people see themselves! If you realize who he is, you will not see him the same way as you once did. If you recognize who he is, you will never see yourself the same way again. If you know who he is, you will never see me as a symbol of death. Instead, you will see the cross as a symbol of life.

I bragged in the fact that I could break the spirit, soul and body of any man. Jesus in turn has broken my braggadocio. He has crushed my conceitedness. He has disarmed my disdain. He has erased my ego. He has negated my nerve. Jesus the Christ has changed the cross!

I am the cross and I held Jesus to his death, so that humanity could have eternal life!

The Sign on the Cross

"And Pilate wrote a title, and put it on the cross. And the writing was JESUS OF NAZARETH THE KING OF THE JEWS."
— John 19:19

"I am the Sign on the Cross!"

It is custom to place a sign on the top of the cross stating the criminal's offense. I was written to be placed on the cross of Jesus. I state, "Jesus the Nazarene, the King of the Jews" in Latin, Greek, and Hebrew.

When the priests read me, they approach Pontius Pilate and asked that I be changed. They would rather me state, "Jesus the Nazarene, He claims to be the King of the Jews", but Pilate wouldn't change me. I remain the way I am originally written.

I am written in Hebrew, Greek and Latin. Anyone walking past the hill will be able to read me. Hebrew and Greek are the languages commonly spoken in this region. Everyone can read me and understand what I say, "Jesus the Nazarene, the King of the Jews."

Many of his followers have called him a king over the last three years. Some have recognized him as a king from long before his ministry began. The scriptures declare that when his birth was announced, three kings came to see him. The kingdom culture is for a king to bow and present a gift in the presence of a greater king. Whenever kings come into contact with one another, the lesser king bows and presents a gift to the greater king. Each of these kings brought a gift and bowed in the presence of Jesus. The first king presented him with gold. This was to represent his royalty and kingly nature. It had been prophesied that he would be a king.

Even dating back before his birth, the angel, Gabriel told Mary, "He shall be great, and will be called the Son of the Most High; and the Lord God will give him the throne of His father David; and he will reign over the house of Jacob forever; and his kingdom will have no end." Gabriel was speaking prophetically about Jesus being a king.

The book of Psalms speaks of the coming king when it states, "But as for Me, I have installed My King upon Zion, My holy mountain. I will surely tell of the decree of the Lord: He said to Me, 'Thou art My Son, today I have begotten Thee.'"

The prophet Zephaniah states, "The King of Israel, the Lord, is in your midst; you will fear disaster no more."

The prophet Zechariah foretells of Jesus' triumphant entry into Jerusalem when he declares, "Rejoice greatly, O daughter of Zion; shout, O daughter of Jerusalem: behold, thy King cometh unto thee: he is just, and having salvation; lowly, and riding upon an ass, and upon a colt, the foal of an ass."

John the Baptist proclaimed the coming Kingdom, saying, "Repent, for the kingdom of heaven is at hand."

After Jesus was baptized and spent time fasting in the wilderness, he was tempted. The scriptures declare that satan offered Jesus the kingdoms of the world if he would bow to him. satan was appealing to Jesus' kingly nature by offering him kingdoms. Jesus refused; a greater king would never bow to a lesser.

The kingdom of God became the central theme of Jesus' teaching and ministry. He declared as did John, "Repent, for the kingdom of heaven is at hand."

The chief accusations against Jesus at his arrest and trial were that he claimed to be king. This is one of the statements that upset the establishment. The priests of the Jewish order were insulted. They were waiting for a king who would come as a military leader or political power. They thought the king would overthrow the Romans and lead the Jewish people to great power. Instead, Jesus spoke of a kingdom of love. Jesus taught that the greatest would be the servant of all in his kingdom. He taught that the kingdom was like a small mustard seed.

The chief priests had Jesus arrested and brought before Pontius Pilate on charges that he claimed to be a king and the son of God. Pilate summoned Jesus, and said to him, "You are the king of the Jews?"

Jesus answered him by saying, "Are you saying this on your own initiative, or did others tell you about me?"

Pilate then said, "I am not a Jew, am I? Your own nation and the chief priest delivered you up to me. What have you done?"

Jesus answered, "My kingdom is not of this world. If my kingdom were of this world, then my servants would be fighting, that I might not be delivered up to the Jews; but as it is, my kingdom is not of this realm."

Pilate then said to him, "So you are a king?"

Jesus responds, "You say correctly that I am a king. For this I have been born and for this I have come into the world, to bear witness to the truth."

The soldiers put purple robes of royalty on him, force a crown of thorns into his head, and give him a mock scepter to ridicule His kingship. When Pilate presented the battered Jesus to the Jews, he stated, "Behold your King!" He then created me; the sign. "Jesus the Nazarene, the King of the Jews."

Now I'm placed at the top of the cross. As they raise the cross, I can see the entire crowd. I see the priests who are hurling slurs at Jesus. They are mocking his kingship. They're yelling at him to come down from the cross. I see the soldiers who are tearing his clothes and casting lots for them. They're yelling, "Hail the king! Hail the king!" I see his mother weeping profusely with some of her friends. I see one of his followers trying to console her.

I look down and see Jesus suffering. He is bleeding all over his body. He is in agony and tremendous pain. His hands are bleeding, his feet are bleeding. He has been whipped and brutally beaten. His head is pouring blood from the crown of thorns. The blood has poured from his body all over the cross and runs onto the ground. Jesus makes no attempt to free himself or get down. He endures.

There are two criminals also being crucified today. There is a criminal on Jesus' left side and a criminal on Jesus' right side. One criminal mocks Jesus like everyone else. He ridicules him and mocks his kingship. He also challenges Jesus to come down from the cross. The other man however recognizes Jesus as king. He may have heard of the prophecies of old. Maybe he is familiar with the story of the kings who bowed at the birth. Maybe he knows the prophecies of Zephaniah and Zechariah. I don't know what he sees in this bloody, beaten man but somehow he recognizes his kingship. He is one of the few in this large crowd who recognizes who he is. He acknowledges him and asks Jesus to remember him when he enters his kingdom.

A true king has the authority to grant access to whomever he chooses. Jesus responds with, "This day you will be with me in paradise." He grants this man access because he is a king. Through all of his pain, anguish, and suffering, he still responds as a king. The prophets recognize Jesus as a king. The three kings recognize Jesus as a king. His followers recognize him as a king. This condemned criminal recognizes him as a king. Now I, the sign on the cross, am fitly placed; for I too recognize Jesus as a king.

Pilate inscribes me because kingship is his crime. The Jews were insulted by me because kingship is his claim. I adorn the cross because kingship is his calling. Jesus proudly accepts me because he is the King of kings.

Jesus with the crown of thorns

The Hammer

> "Carrying the cross by himself, he went to the place called Place of the Skull (in Hebrew, Golgotha). There they nailed him to the cross."
> — John 19:17-18

"I am the Hammer!"

The hammer is the carpenter's favorite tool. No carpenter is ever seen without his hammer. The hammer is the symbol of the trade. Carpenters are defined by their hammer and their skill in constructing with it.

The logo of the carpenter is the hammer. The brand of the carpenter is the hammer. The hammer is the carpenter's best friend. No tool comes between a carpenter and his hammer. Our friendship spans his lifetime for as long as he bears witness to the craft, I am there for him.

Jesus grew up as a carpenter. Carpentry was the family business. His father Joseph is a carpenter. Joseph taught the trade to Jesus and gave me to him. I remember when Jesus first picked me up to learn to use me. Every young carpenter has to learn to use a hammer. Jesus has used me many times since we met. He skillfully would use me to press nails through wood. He sometimes would tap wood into place using me. He had a variety of uses for me as most carpenters do.

Jesus became so well skilled with me that he began to be recognized within the carpentry profession. When he began to minister here in Jerusalem, many asked, "Is this not the carpenter; Joseph's son?" This is because they knew him by his profession, by his family business; as a carpenter. They knew him through his hammer and this is how they identified him.

Once Jesus began his ministry, he stopped carrying me around. He left the art of carpentry behind. He left the wood, the nails, and me behind to pursue his ministry. Jesus went from being a carpenter to being a caregiver. He went from being an entrepreneur to being an evangelist. He went from being a professional to being a preacher. Jesus left his trade to become a teacher. He left me, the hammer, to become a healer.

I haven't seen Jesus since he left the trade. That was three years ago. How ironic now that we cross paths again! I can honestly say that I've missed him. No carpenter leaves their hammer for another trade but Jesus had to do what was best for him at the time. His destiny in ministry was calling him to pursue and now his destiny has led him back to me; his lifelong friend.

When the soldiers select me today, I don't know what I am to be used for. I have been used to build houses and wells. I have been used to build all manner of furniture from tables to chairs. This time however, they take me out of the carpenter's workplace. I won't be used inside the city proper. Instead, I'm being carried to the outskirts of town. When we arrive at the destination, I see the wood and I see the nails. There are two large beam structures and three iron spikes.

The tools of carpentry are here. Then I see him.

Jesus! The former carpenter! I barely recognize him through the blood that is all over his body. But I know it's him. I'd know those hands anywhere. His face is so badly beaten that he's unrecognizable, yet I know him by his hands. He's stripped almost naked and his body is severely scourged but I know him by those hands.

Having not seen him in three years, I ache for him now. Much has changed since he last held me. His popularity and hatred grew at the same time. It is evidenced by the large crowd of onlookers that he has both enemies and friends who have come to witness this spectacle. I had no idea that I would not only be a witness but a participant in the killing of my friend.

The large wooden structure is placed on the ground and Jesus is being made to lay his back upon it. They stretch him across the horizontal beam and pull his arms in either direction. The soldiers bring me close along with the nails.

I realize now what is happening. The very utensils that Jesus once used to make a living are now being used to take his life! I, along with the wood and the nails are being used to kill him. He built with us, now we're breaking him.

The soldiers place the first nail into the palm of his hand and raise me high. When I come slamming down upon the nail, I feel the impact and the pressure drive the nail through his hand. I feel the vibration as I drive the nail. The nail goes through his hand easily but it takes a few strokes from me to push through the wood. Each time I come down upon the nail, I feel the pressure of the impact pass through his hand. I can feel his anguish. I can sense his pain.

No human is supposed to take nails driven through his hand with a hammer, but he does.

The second nail is placed into his other palm. I slam down on this nail like I did the first one. I push the nail right through his flesh. I hear Jesus cry out as I push the nail through his hand. The hand that once held me and learned to use me is now pierced through by a nail that I helped to push.

No human is supposed to take nails driven through his hand with a hammer, but he does.

Blood is now pouring through both of his hands. Jesus' hands are so damaged that they will never hold me again. He will never be able to create another table or chair. I've helped to destroy his hands. He used me and now I'm being used against him.

The soldiers line his feet up to be fastened to the vertical beam. It takes twice the amount of hits by me to get through both of his feet. Each time I strike a nail, the sound of two pieces of metal slamming together resonates and feels like the worst type of pain on earth. Each stroke brings a new level of pain and agony.

No human is supposed to take nails driven through his feet with a hammer, but he does.

Blood is now pouring from his feet. His blood is all

over the wooden cross beams and the nails. His blood is pouring onto the ground.

The soldiers turn the cross completely over so that I can secure the nails from the other side. They slam me down on the end of the first nail. It bends immediately and fastens to the other side of the cross. They do the same to the second and the third nail. Now the nails are secure. I've totally fastened them to the cross.

As I'm tossed aside, I look up at my friend. He is hanging. He is bleeding. He is praying. He is dying. I think back to Jesus as a child. I remember his small hands becoming adjusted to me. I remember his first swing. I remember his first completed project. I remember him as a teenager when he had learned to use me so well that he could build or break with one thrust. I remember Jesus as an adult, and how he was so skilled as a carpenter and used it to provide for his family. I will never let go of those good memories, nor will I relinquish what I witnessed today.

I am the hammer, the carpenter's favorite tool. I was once used to create; now I am used to destroy. I was once used to build; now I am used to tear down. I was once used for construction, now I am used for destruction. I was once used by Jesus the carpenter, now I am being used for Jesus' crucifixion.

The crucifixion

The Nails

> "Carrying the cross by himself, he went to the place called Place of the Skull (in Hebrew, Golgotha). There they nailed him to the cross."
> — John 19:17-18

"I am the Nail!"

Nails that are my size are not common. I am created to hold together large structures and beams. I'm made of iron with an extremely pointed tip. My edges are sharpened. I am a spike that is strong enough to keep anything tightly fit together.

The Roman fortresses have workshops where the blacksmiths fashion metal items needed by the army. They've made over seven tons of nails in times of war. To make me, an iron ore is heated with carbon. I'm then fashioned into the shape of square rods and left to cool. The metal produced is wrought iron. After reheating, the blacksmith cuts me and hammers all four of my sides to form a point.

When I was selected on this day, I did not know why. Was it to secure a beam? Was it to firm a structure? I never know my purpose until I am hammered into place. When I was picked up by the Romans earlier this morning, I had no idea what I was to be used for. I'm always ready to secure. Regardless of what I am to be used for, I am always prepared.

The Roman soldiers carry me to the hill where the cross is laying. It is a huge wooden structure. It is a large cross beam. I can easily hold a structure like this together. I'm prepared to be hammered into place.

But now I see him. Jesus of Nazareth. Jesus the carpenter. Jesus the criminal.

The soldiers lay him onto the cross and place his feet together. They stretched out both of his arms as far as they can be stretched. They open both of his hands. I then realize that I'm not going to be used for architecture. I am not going to be wedged between two pieces of wood. I'm not being used to support the beam. My purpose today is not to hold the large structure together. Those reasons aren't my purpose at all.

The soldiers place me inside the palm of his hand. These are the same hands he rose to calm the raging sea. These are the same hands he used to feed the multitude with the loaves and fish. These are the same hands he used to heal blind Bartimaeus. These are the same hands he used to draw in the sand.

Jesus used these hands to wash the disciples' feet. He used these hands to break the bread with his disciples. Jesus used these hands to pass the cup of his blood. Now I am preparing to pierce his hands and fasten him to a cross!

One of the soldiers holds me in place and raises the hammer high. He brings it upon my head with all of his might. When the hammer slams down upon me, I break through the palm of Jesus and his blood pours out. I can feel the pain ripple through each finger. I can feel the agonizing pain shoot across his palm; yet, Jesus accepts it. He accepts me tearing through him. He accepts me securing him to the wooden cross. He accepts it, one nail at a time.

Another soldier places me in the palm of his other hand. Jesus willingly opens his palm as they place my pointed edge against his skin. Once again, the hammer comes slamming down. I easily break through his flesh and his blood pours out. I can feel the pain ripple through each finger. I can feel the agonizing pain shoot across his palm. Jesus accepts it. He accepts me tearing through him. He accepts me securing him to the wooden cross. He accepts it, one nail at a time.

After I pierced each hand and fastened him to hang, they also placed me at his feet. The same feet that walked on water. The same feet that walked the streets of Jerusalem and the shores of Galilee. These are the feet that the woman washed with her tears. These are the feet that marched into the synagogue and drove out the merchants and traders. These feet walked right up to the tomb where they laid Lazarus just before he was called forth from the dead. Now I am piercing each foot and securing them together to the cross.

A soldier places one of Jesus' feet on top of the other. Another soldier places my edge on top of his foot. The hammer comes slamming down upon me and I easily break through both feet. When I break through his foot, blood pours out. I sense the pain go through each of his toes. I feel the tremendous pain ripple through each foot and up his legs. Jesus accepts it. He accepts me ripping through his feet. He accepts being fastened to a wooden cross. Jesus accepts it, one nail at a time.

    I pierce straight through both of his hands and both of his feet. I feel the wood on the other side of him. I am pushed so hard by the hammer that I enter the wood. With each blow from the hammer, I go deeper into the wood. My narrow end is now piercing through wood while my wider edge is tearing through the hands and feet of Jesus. With a final push, I break through the other side of the wood. Blood is pouring all over me and dripping out of the other side of the cross. Blood is pouring so fast from the three wounds that a small pool is forming on the ground. Yet, he still accepts this torture and doesn't fight back.

    The soldiers turn the huge wooden structure over in order to bend my edges into place. This is to securely fasten Jesus to the cross. They bang each edge with a solid blow and I am now fastened; I'm now holding Jesus into place.

    Nails that are my size can easily hold large structures. That's what we're created for. That's what we're molded for. To hold a man to wood is an easy assignment. My cast iron is much stronger than a man's hands and feet. I was prepared for something much stronger than this.

    The soldiers stand the cross up for all to see him. When the cross drops into the hole that the soldiers dug, I feel Jesus' body jerk forward and I hold tight. He is securely fastened and cannot break free from my hold. I am the element of the crucifixion holding him in place. I am the element of the crucifixion making sure he doesn't come down. Without me holding him in place, Jesus would come down.

One of the onlookers from the crowd yells at him, "Jesus could perform miracles and save others! Why doesn't he save himself?" Another person yells at him, "If you come down off the cross, we will believe you and follow you!" A priest then mocks him, "If you are the son of God, why don't you come down off the cross and save yourself?" I think about what the people in the crowd are saying. I listen to how they are mocking and cursing him. They're saying that he performed miracles. They're yelling out that he claims to be the son of God.

Then I remember! I was a part of the building where the wedding was in Cana. I saw Jesus turn water into wine!

I was a part of the structure of the home in Capernaum where the young man laid ill and was close to death. His father went to Jesus and asked for healing. I saw that young man become healed, the very hour his father spoke with Jesus!

I was in the synagogue in Capernaum on the Sabbath when Jesus came in to teach. I was amazed, as were the people at his teaching, because he taught them as one who had authority, not as the teachers of the law. Just then a man who was possessed by an impure spirit screamed, "What do you want with us, Jesus of Nazareth? Have you come to destroy us? I know who you are, the Holy One of God!" Jesus then answered loudly, "Be quiet! Come out of him!" I saw the impure spirit shake the man violently and come out of him.

I was in the structure of Simon Peter's house. His mother was inside and was sick with fever. I saw Jesus rebuke the fever and immediately she was made well and began to wait on Jesus and the disciples!

I was also in the structure of Simon Peter's boat when Jesus entered it. The fishermen had been attempting to catch fish all night. Jesus instructed them to cast out again. Peter, being a skilled fisherman, knew that there was no chance of catching anything, especially on the side of the boat to which Jesus instructed them to cast. I saw the extraordinary catch! There were so many fish that the nets began to break and the men had to call other boats for assistance!

I was in the building where the centurion's son was. This young man was so sick that he was close to death. I saw this young man miraculously healed at the same time Jesus spoke to the centurion and told him that his son would be healed!

I was in the beam of the roof when the four men tore the roof off to get their paralyzed friend to Jesus. They lowered him down and Jesus forgave him of his sins and healed him! I saw that young man take up his bed and walk!

I was nailed into the wall of the synagogue when the man entered with the withered hand. I saw Jesus heal the man, even though it was on the Sabbath and against religious law to work on the Sabbath!

I was holding together the town gate in the city of Nain. There was a large crowd of weeping people, crying over a dead child who was being carried out of the city. His widow mother was weeping. I saw Jesus bring the child back to life and give him back to his mother!

I had a difficult time holding the boat together as the storm raged against me. Jesus was on the boat with his disciples but was asleep. I saw them wake him up and I saw him stand on the edge of the boat. He raised his hands and said. "Peace be still!" I saw the sea quiet down and become peaceful at his command!

I was in the architecture of Jairus' house. He went to Jesus to beg for his daughter's healing. His daughter died while Jesus was on the way to see her. Jesus told the mourners at the house that the child was merely sleeping. I saw them laugh at Jesus. I then witnessed Jesus put them out and bring the child back to life!

There are so many other times I witnessed miracles. I saw him walk on water! I saw him heal Bartimaeus! I watched him bring Lazarus back to life! I was in the well when Jesus told that women all the men she was with and all she had ever done! Miracle after miracle after miracle! I saw Jesus do the impossible! I saw him do the improbable! I saw him do what could not be done! I then realized it isn't me keeping him on the cross. He has the power to come down! He can come down from the cross whenever he wants. It isn't me at all keeping him here, it is love!

I thought that I was the only thing keeping him on the cross. I thought that I was the only thing securing him to the cross. I thought I was the one that made sure he did not come down. No. I realize now that it is his love that holds him there. It is his compassion that keeps him there. It is his desire to save mankind that secures him there.

Yes, the pain I caused fastened him there, but his love has kept him there.

The Sponge

"Now there was set a vessel full of vinegar: and they filled a sponge with vinegar, and put it upon hyssop, and put it to his mouth."
— John 19:29

"I am the Sponge!"

I am the element of the crucifixion that is least spoken of. I'm not referred to nor spoken of. I've been misunderstood and glanced over. People don't know a lot about me even though I'm spoken of earlier in the Bible. Psalm 69 says, "They gave me also gall for my meat; and in my thirst they gave me vinegar to drink." These were offered to Jesus on me, the sponge.

I was taken to the hill by one of the Roman soldiers. It was not unusual for me to attend a crucifixion. Many times I'm filled with water and used to pour the water over the head of the criminal. Other times I'm filled with wine and offered to the criminal to drink before he dies. This crucifixion seemed like others that I have attended until I saw Jesus.

I watched the soldiers lay the cross on the ground. I saw them push Jesus onto the cross. I watched them nail his hands and his feet to the cross. They raised the cross and set it into a hole in the ground. He hung between two other criminals who were also condemned to die. Many in the crowd yelled at him. Some who were there were crying, some were laughing. I've never seen a crucifixion like this.

After several hours passed, one of the soldiers retrieved me and carried me close to the cross. I was placed into a cup and receive the vinegar inside the cup. I immediately recognize the gall and myrrh inside the cup. The vinegar has been mixed with gall. I become full and I'm placed on the end of a spear to reach his mouth. I'm placed so close to his mouth that I touch his bloody lips. He tastes the vinegar but refuses to drink any more. The soldier holding the spear pushes me a few more times toward his face. Each time Jesus turns his head away. He refuses to drink from me.

I've never seen a criminal refuse to drink.

The soldier takes me off the long spear and rings me out onto the ground. I let go of the mixture of vinegar and gall until it all pours out of me.

I'm very intrigued with this Jesus criminal now. I've never seen a prisoner beaten so badly. I've never seen a prisoner reviled so harshly by an on looking crowd. Now he refuses to drink. Who is this man and why does he seem so special?

Close to an hour later, I'm filled with vinegar again. This time there is no gall or myrrh. I'm filled with acetum which is a thin, tart, sour wine diluted with water that soldiers drink often. This mixture is often called vinegar and is so strong that it heightens the senses. This is why they use water to dilute it. The more water used, the weaker the solution. As they fill me up, I don't recognize the presence of any water at all.

This time I'm placed on the spear and presented to Jesus again. The soldier raises the spear and pushes me against his mouth. He takes a taste of the vinegar and drinks. He clinches his teeth as the liquid solution enters his mouth. Jesus turns his head away and wants no more.

As I'm lowered down, I begin to understand. Jesus refuses me the first time because I contained gall and myrrh. This mixture would have deadened the pain that he was suffering. That's what gall is used for. It lowers the senses and the person feels less pain. Gall has always been used as a pain reliever. Instead, he drinks the pure acetum solution which will heighten his senses and cause him to be fully aware of the torture he is experiencing. The vinegar makes him feel the pain even more.

Jesus wants to feel every ounce of the pain. He wants to experience this torture. He refuses any relief.

He has accepted his destiny. The Bible says in the book of Hebrews, that for the joy that is set before him, he endured the full extent of the cross. That is what he is doing. I realize the reason he is doing this. He is doing this to fulfill the words of the prophet in Psalms. Jesus' task is to do the will of his Father by fulfilling the prophecies declared about him in the scriptures. He cannot die until he has fulfilled every prophecy.

The prophets said that he would become flesh

and walk amongst men. The prophets said that he would be born of a virgin. The prophets said that he would be born in a stable. The prophets said that the government will be upon his shoulder and his name shall be called Wonderful, Counselor, the mighty God, the everlasting Father, the Prince of Peace. The prophets said that he would be wounded for the transgressions of men. The prophets said that he would be bruised for the iniquities of men. The prophets said that the chastisement of men's peace would be upon him.

Jesus is obligated to fulfill the many things said about him. He owed it to the prophets. There were many prophecies said and he fulfills them all. Tasting the vinegar from me was the only prophecy that He had yet to fulfill. Before he dies, he fulfills the words of the prophet David; "they gave me also gall for my meat; and in my thirst they gave me vinegar to drink."

After he takes the vinegar, he says, "It is finished!" and he drops his head.

I'm the last thing that comes into contact with Jesus before he dies. I'm the last of the prophetic words spoken about him. He cannot cry out that it is finished until he drinks from me. He cannot give up his spirit until he drinks from me. He cannot complete his mission until he drinks from me.

Jesus came to save mankind. Jesus came to take away the sins of the world according to the scriptures. Jesus also came to satisfy the prophets. Now that he has taken from me, the prophets are satisfied.

The Spear

> *"But one of the soldiers with a spear pierced his side, and forthwith came there out blood and water."*
> — John 19:34

"I am the Spear!"

I am the final tool used in the Crucifixion. One of the Roman soldiers stands at the foot of the cross and looks up at Jesus who has been crucified. He holds me in his hand. He wants to see if Jesus is truly dead or not. The custom is to break the criminal's legs so he would die sooner. When a criminal hangs for many hours, they find it hard to breathe.

The man's lungs slowly collapse and sink and he pushes himself up for air. By breaking his legs, he can no longer push himself up for air. The criminal begins to gasp and heave. He coughs as he cries in anguish. He screams as loud as he can until his scream is barely a whisper. The pain of losing your breath is worse than the pain of broken legs. This is crucifixion.

I was carried to the crucifixion by the soldier and I watched Jesus the entire time. He struggled up the hill carrying the weight of the cross. The soldiers laughed at him, kicked him, cursed him, and pushed him around from the moment I saw him. He never fought back nor spoke against any of them. He bore the weight of the cross until he could bear it no longer.

Now I watch quietly as Jesus is nailed and lifted. I watch as the other soldiers gamble for his clothes. I stand by and watch as the Jewish priests insult him. I watch as some of his followers surround the cross crying.

I've been to several crucifixions and been through several battles with the Romans. I've seen gruesome events when men fight. I've witnessed tortures and crucifixions, which were brutal in nature. Yet in all of the events that I have witnessed with the Romans, I have never seen a man take the punishment that Jesus has. He is covered in bruises, cuts, and blood; his face is disfigured. He has been whipped, beaten, punched, kicked, spat on, cursed, and finally nailed to a cross. Furthermore, he suffers as it is the hottest part of the day and the sun is beaming down as he hangs.

Jesus doesn't say much. He speaks to a disciple at the foot of the cross. He speaks to one of the criminals hanging next to him who is also condemned to die. At this point however, something strange occurs. He begins to look toward the sky and speak to the clouds. "God! My God! Why have you forsaken me?" Everyone seems confused at this statement by him. He says again to the sky, "Father forgive them for they know not what they do." Once again, everyone is confused at his sayings.

The other criminals are now gasping for air and pushing themselves up by their feet for air. Jesus is not doing that though. He is hanging and bleeding all over the cross and the ground. He musters what strength he still has and lifts his head. He says, "Father, into your hands I commend my spirit," and his head drops. Immediately the ground begins to shake and the sky darkens. Everyone begins to look around frantically at what is happening. The soldiers begin to yell commands and one of the soldiers swings his club to break the legs of one of the criminals. The man, who can barely breathe screams in agony. The same soldier quickly approaches the other criminal who begins to scream before he is hit. When the club shatters the bone in his legs, he begins to yell even louder. He now approaches Jesus to break his legs but looks at him instead. Jesus appears to be dead so he doesn't swing. He instead backs away, staring at Jesus.

The next thing that happens would change my perspective of Jesus and his purpose. It would change my thoughts about crucifixions in general. It would change me forever.

The soldier that is holding me approaches Jesus and with one push, thrusts me into his side. He wants to insure that Jesus is truly dead since his legs were not broken to initiate suffocation. This act by this Roman soldier has become one of the signature elements of the crucifixion of Jesus. Many have become familiar with this aspect of the crucifixion of Jesus. Many have heard what happened to him when I pierced his side. Many have heard that blood and water ran out from his side once he was pierced. That is exactly what happened to him but what about what happened to me? No one has ever considered what happened to me.

When I was shoved through his side and I pierced him, I saw his heart! I saw the heart of God! I saw the reason he endured the whip and endured the nails and the crown of thorns. What seemed like a split second to most became an eternity for me. While inside Jesus,

I saw his love for the first man, Adam. Adam walked with God and was close to God's heart. Adam was close to the heartbeat of God. Adam however sinned and fell away from God. There became a separation between man and God's heart. I saw the longing to get back to man when I saw Jesus' heart.

When God instructed his people, the children of Israel to approach him at Mount Sinai, he set a boundary all around the mountain. His instructions were that no one from the children of Israel could pass the boundary and survive. You could come close, but you could not pass through the boundary. Men could approach, but no one could break through. Men could get close, but no one could break through. Men could draw near, but no one could break through. This was because of sin. Sin separated man from the heart of God. Man did not have a way to get back to the heart of God.

When I broke through the rib cage of Jesus, I became the breakthrough! I broke through the flesh and saw his heart! The crowd that had gathered saw blood and water but I saw God's heart. The Roman soldier holding me saw the Son of God for he said, "Truly this man was the Son of God!" but I saw God's heart.

God's heart is for his people to receive a breakthrough. Just as I came near the heart of God, he wants his people to draw near to his heart. He wants his people to see what I saw. I saw his heart, his love, his compassion, and how much he cares. He wants the same for his people. He desires for his people to see what I saw; his undying and unmatched love.

Gestas Thief

> *"And with him they crucify two thieves; the one on his right hand, and the other on his left."*
> — Mark 15:27

> *"For the preaching of the cross is to them that perish foolishness; but unto us which are saved it is the power of God".*
> – 1 Corinthians 1:18

"I am a Gestas!"

I am a thief. I am criminally minded. It has been said and written that he who does not teach his son a trade is raising a thief. I am living proof for I have thought the thoughts of a thief my entire life.

Everything I accomplish is for me.

Earning possessions does not prove worthiness. Do you deserve what you have?

If I take from you, I am more powerful than you are.

I never consider the desire of others. To do so is a sign of weakness.

These are the thoughts of a thief. These are my thoughts.

I've never passed on an opportunity to steal from someone. If an opportunity presents itself, I take it. For this reason, I have become renowned in Jerusalem, Gestas; the criminal thief.

For as many times as I have expressed myself as a thief, there is a larger and more popular thief than even I. I believe the Roman Empire is the largest and most organized criminal organization in the world. I knew and understood this to be true when I became a man and began to understand the irony in which the world works.

The Romans force us to pay taxes to them so that we can live in a land that we already own. Why am I charged to live in Jerusalem? Why am I charged to reside in my home? They would like to charge us for the air we breathe! They are the true criminals. They are the thieves. I've stolen from them. I don't care. I have taken from them with no remorse. I hate them and my hatred began to drive me into the man I am. I have always thought the thoughts of a thief. Now I couple that with the hatred of the true thieves.

Dismas and I have been in a band of thieves for years. Our people know us well. The Romans know us well. We have both made our mark as criminals. Both the Jews and the Romans were equally pleased to pronounce a sentence of death upon us I'm sure.

While in prison, I met another career criminal named Barabbas. He feels the same way that I do about Rome and their oppression of the Jewish nation. They have bullied us. They have walked our streets like they own those streets. Most Jews are afraid of the Romans. Even the so-called Jewish religious leadership is afraid. Cowards! Barabbas is known to have led a revolt against the Romans. Had he been equipped like they are with weapons and garrison, he would have prevailed.

    I admire Barabbas, but we don't think alike. He thinks as a criminal. I think as a thief. My thoughts are much more self-motivated and self-serving. He would like to overthrow Rome to achieve the power status of a military domination. The Jews are the select people and we are supposed to rule. Barabbas would like to murder, kill and steal in order to achieve the coveted position we should be standing in. I simply have thoughts of a thief. The basis of my thoughts is to become wealthy. Nonetheless, Barabbas is a dynamic individual who has caused a stir in this prison dungeon.

    Barabbas has become somewhat of a leader amongst thieves. He asks the others what they have been arrested for. Most have stolen something and been arrested and imprisoned. A few do not answer him and chose silence. I can tell they are afraid of him. I can see fear in the eyes of a man; it is a trait of a true thief. When I am questioned, I proudly confess that I have stolen from hundreds but have yet to enjoy the perfect score. Perfection would be the power of Pilate and the gold of the temple inner sanctum. I have stolen the cloak off the back of a traveling man and proudly worn his clothes the same afternoon. I state that I am a thief without the weakness of guilt or remorse. I am a thief who is proud to be a criminal. I am a thief without fear or doubt. I take what I want. I do not apologize and I would look my accuser in the face and steal again.

    Dismas laughs as he hears my explanation of our exploits. Some of the others criminals laugh and murmur amongst themselves when I am finished. They are men of Jewish decent, shackled and chained with the iron of Rome. Men who are linked to each other or chained to the wall are discussing the particular circumstances which led to their demise. These are the only men I have met where I have not considered taking what they have for these men have nothing but one another. Hence, they are somewhat worthless to me. Without material possessions, what am I to do? What can I gain besides your words which can be forgotten in a minute's time? I am a thief by nature and I think the thoughts of a thief. True thieves think of themselves only. Gestas thinks of the best interest of Gestas. Rome thinks of itself as the world's most powerful empire. Why? Because Romans are thieves and think as true criminals.

The day that the soldiers came and took Barabbas was a shock and surprise to us all. No one knew if he was to be crucified or scourged. The next thing I knew, more soldiers came and they began to unshackle both Dismas and I. I didn't know what was happening. I swallowed any fear that may have risen inside and followed the directions of the soldier criminals. The sunlight was so bright when they took me up from the prison that I had to keep my eyes closed for several minutes. I did not see nor hear Barabbas. I don't know what they have done with him. I didn't realize that a sentence of death would be executed today. I was then introduced to my tool of torture. I was pushed down onto the very cross that I would carry and be hammered to. My fate is sealed. Today is my final day on earth. I, along with Dismas and another man who I do not know are to be murdered today by the Romans!

The other man is bleeding profusely. It's a wonder he is not dead yet. He has thorns sticking from his head and blood soaking through his garments. I have never seen a man bleed as much as he has, even in the murders I have witnessed. I hear his name chanted from the massive crowd that has seemed to gather to see him die...his name is Jesus.

Jesus! I have heard of him! He is the Nazarene! He has preached that he is God's son. I have heard that the Pharisees have called him a criminal because he says that he is the Messiah. Is that a crime? No, I am a criminal. Barabbas is a criminal. Dismas is a criminal. Jesus is an activist. He doesn't deserve the title of criminal.

A massive crowd has gathered to witness the crucifixion of this Jesus. I've never seen such emotion for a man. There are women weeping and screaming. There are Pharisees in the crowd walking alongside. They are keeping quiet. They are mostly cowards. There are soldiers kicking him and beating his body mercilessly. There are soldiers holding back the crowd. It seems as some are trying to spit on him and some are yelling. As much as I honor the thief that I am, I do not envy Jesus for the punishment they are inflicting upon him. I am in tremendous pain but my pain is a weak comparison to what he has gone through. Although he doesn't deserve the title of thief as the honor I see it as, who deserves such punishment as he is taking? A man who makes false accusations about himself?

He falls three times so the Romans grab a man to help him. None of the soldiers would help. As weak as he is, they still forcibly push him onward. Jesus never fights back. I don't know what kind of Messiah he claims to be but weakness is not a trait of a true Messiah or criminal. He isn't worthy of either title.

We reach the top of the hill where we will breathe our last breaths. Dismas is exhausted and bleeding. Only my screams of pain drown his out as we are nailed to our respective crosses. I have never felt such pain. Incredibly sharp pains run through my entire body as the spike breaks through the flesh of my palm. I immediately scream at my loudest. I scream not only because of the intense and immediate pain, but also because I've come to the realization that these hands will never rob again. My hands have been my trademark to how I've made a living for myself. Not the hands of a carpenter or builder, yet a skill nonetheless.

They nail my feet, and I can no longer take the pain. I'd rather die right now then face the pain I am in. I look at Dismas who is hanging his head as his cross is raised. They raise my cross and drop it into the hole in the ground and I feel my body lean forward as if I would be thrown to the ground from this high place. The nails have kept me from falling forward which only causes more pain.

I look down at the crowd that seems to have tripled in size, all to see this Jesus fellow. His cross is between Dismas and me. I can look to my left and see them both. A man being crucified for being, thinking, and acting as a thief. Another man being crucified for saying that he is the long awaited Messiah. The Romans mock us and the Pharisees mock Jesus. These are the men who should be hanging, not us! Cowards and criminals!

One of the Pharisees challenges Jesus to come down off the cross. He yells that he saved others but cannot save himself. Another mocks if he is the true son of God, why not prove it by coming down off the cross!

I look at Jesus. He is not speaking back to them at all. He is not answering. What kind of man can take such abuse? What kind of man can have such things screamed at him and not respond? This man is supposed to be the Messiah. I look at a sign that is on the top of his cross. It says "Jesus of Nazareth the King of the Jews." This Jesus is supposed to be our king. He is the Messiah, or so he claims. If he is, he has the power to not only come down from the cross but to also get Dismas and I down as well! If he can do that, we can leave Jerusalem. We can go to the shores of Galilee! We can leave Rome altogether! Imagine the power we can have! Imagine the possibilities! Get me down! Stop this incredible pain!

"Are you not the Messiah?" I scream at him. "Save yourself and us!"

Instead of Jesus responding to me, Dismas does! "Have you no fear of God? We have been condemned justly, for the sentence we received corresponds to our crimes, but this man has done nothing criminal! He has done nothing wrong!" Dismas then looks at Jesus and speaks to him as I just did. "Jesus, remember me when you come into your kingdom!" Jesus picks up his head and turns toward Dismas. I can hear Jesus clearly even though he isn't facing me. "Amen, I say to you, today you will be with me in Paradise." Jesus told Dismas that he would take him to paradise. What paradise? He can't even come down from this torture!

He can't even save himself! He can't do anything for me! I think the thoughts of a thief and I want my freedom or I have no use for this Jesus! He is no thief, he is no criminal! Instead, he is a fraud!

My pain is unbearable; so much so that my mind is hallucinating and my mouth is starting to foam. In an instance, I see the crowd begin to shake and fall as if the ground they stand on is moving. The hill is rocking back and forth and people are falling on top of one another. I know this is a dying man's dream! The Pharisees are running for their lives. One of the soldiers grabs a wooden club and swings it at my legs. I watch the club swing and crack my legs like glass! My body drops and my hands feel like they're going to rip from the nails! I yell in pain and I curse the soldier! The pain is now unbearable and I can't breathe as well!

I can't push myself up for air. I'm coughing and crying. I'm trying to pull myself up with my hands but I can't. I can't get enough air. I'm choking! I can't inhale to scream again… my lungs are burning now… my legs are twisted and broken… I can't feel my feet… I can't inhale… I can't inhale… this is… the death of… a thie…

Darkness.

Opening my eyes and I'm falling! Terror and darkness! I'm falling!

Somebody help me! Help me! Help me! I'm falling! Somebody help me!

Fire! Intense fire! I'm on fire! No! No! No! Nooooooooooooooooooo! Heeeeeeelp meeeeee! Pleeeeeeeeease!

Dismas the Thief

"And with him they crucify two thieves; the one on his right hand, and the other on his left."
— Mark 15:27

"For the preaching of the cross is to them that perish foolishness; but unto us which are saved it is the power of God."
— 1 Corinthians 1:18

"I am Dismas!"

I've lived the life of a thief. I think the thoughts of a thief. I know that I have the heart of a thief; stealing is the first thought I have in most situations. I have always found it easy to steal. I laugh at those who are not cautious enough to secure their belongings.

I find it too easy to steal from them at times. Instead, I'd rather steal from a worthy target. Someone who thinks they are secure and protected. I find ways to steal from them. I am a thief at heart.

When I select a target to steal from, my heart begins to race. My palms become sweaty and my mouth waters. I remember once following a target an extra mile and a half from the direction that I was traveling because the temptation was great to steal from him.

At times, I feel that I can't help myself. Being a thief has become a part of me. It's simply the way that I think and behave. I will always think this way. I am a thief by nature.

I've stolen from travelers on the road. Many of them travel without the aid of protection. Many travel alone. These are the easiest of targets, for they are not prepared for an ambush on the side of the road. I've gained a true spoil from these types of victims. I have stolen from homes. Although most families possess the same types of items, I will take them. It's not the item that drives me to steal. It's the thrill of doing it. It's the rush of being in someone's home when they are not there. It's the feeling I get when I am doing something that I am not supposed to do. This is what ultimately drives me to steal. It is an inner compulsion that grows stronger with each theft. I cannot deny this passion. I cannot portray myself in another light other than the man that I am. I am a thief by nature, by heart and desire.

I've committed thousands of crimes. Although I have lost count of the exact number of crimes long ago, I specifically remember each one as if the event happened yesterday. I remember a band of us plotting to steal from a certain wealthy traveler on the road. We set an ambush ahead of him and had men in waiting behind him. When we pounced on him, he was completely overwhelmed. He traveled with forty drachmas worth of currency, food and water. He also had fine Egyptian linen which I knew would go for a hefty price with the traders. His theft was swift. He was vulnerable. He was surprised and unarmed. My adrenaline was racing as if I had just run my fastest. I was wealthier when I left him than when I attacked him for we had taken all of his belongings.

Of all of the crimes I have committed that are too numerous to count, there is one crime to any thief that he will never forget…the one in which he is apprehended. The final crime. This crime plays over in the mind of a criminal a thousand times every day. This is the one thing that ravishes his mind while he is imprisoned. Could things have been done differently? Did greed overtake him and the desire for one more hit overcome strategic planning? What mistakes did he make that led to his capture and arrest? What level of crime would leave a man sentenced to crucifixion?

My band of brothers consisted of a group of thieves that were notoriously known for our crimes. Until the time that I met such a group of men, I thought I was the only man with the urges and desires that I possess. Never did I imagine that there were more men like me with the addiction to criminal activity. When we discussed a target or an opportunity, each man's eye would sparkle. I could literally see their calculated thoughts as we discussed the purse and the reward of the theft. It seems as if we left no stone unturned in the planning of our capers. The one aspect we never spoke of, probably the most important aspect, was being apprehended; we assumed it would never happen. When it did, it took all of us by surprise.

We were quickly thrown into chains within the Roman prison. Due to the number of crimes we were alleged to have committed, we were thrown into the lowest part of the prison. This area of the prison held the worst criminals; those that committed murder or who conspired against Rome. One of the worst alleged criminals in chains was Barabbas. He was supposedly an insurrectionist against the Roman government and was sentenced to crucifixion.

The soldiers entered the prison and took Barabbas with them. We thought it was his day to be crucified. It wasn't until I was taken along with Gestas and given our crucifixion crosses to bear that I found out that Barabbas had been released and we were being crucified for our crimes. The custom of the Jews is to release one prisoner on death row in honor of Passover. Barabbas had become that prisoner.

There was another prisoner who was led along the path with Gestas and I. I had never seen him before, yet because of him; no attention was paid to me or Gestas. Everyone screamed at this prisoner. All of Jerusalem had come to witness this man's crucifixion. His name is Jesus.

He struggled with his cross. Each time he stumbled and fell, the soldiers kicked him severely. He had been beaten worse than we were. He was bloodied unlike a man I had ever seen, dead or alive. For a moment I felt sorry for him. What could he have possibly done to deserve a worse fate than ours?

The pain that I felt in my hands and feet from being nailed to the cross was so severe that I invited death to take me. I had never felt such excruciating pain. I cried out with my loudest cry as the pain traveled from my hands through my spine and all the way to my toes. My head throbbed from the pain of the spike being pushed through both my feet.

As they raised my cross in the air, my pain became so great that I could barely breathe. I looked at Gestas who was also screaming in anguish. I then glanced at the man Jesus who was between Gestas and I. On this man's head were thorns that caused his head to bleed severely. I had never seen anything like this! All of the attention was focused on him. I looked into the crowd and recognized men of renown. The Levitical priesthood had attended this man's execution. One, stepping forward, made a declaration toward Jesus out loud; "You saved others! Why not come down from that cross and save yourself!" This is the point that I recognize who this man is. This is the man who is known for bringing a dead man to life. This is the man who is known for dealing with the crazy man and sending his spirit into pigs. Word of this man's deeds has traveled much farther than he has. I know this man! I have never met him, but I know this man!

As my life and my criminal deeds flash before my eyes, I hang in agony. I can barely breathe as I continually push myself up for air. No one is paying attention to my cries as the crowd either cries or screams at Jesus. They scream at him to get down and save himself. Some are laughing at him. Some have even spit toward him. He says nothing back toward any of them in anger. I turn my head to get a good look at him and he is gazing upward into the sky. He then speaks to the sky and says, "Father forgive them for they know not what they are doing." Jesus just asked God to forgive the men that have been cursing him, beating him, and casting lots for his clothes.

How could he do such a thing? I wanted to kill every last one of these wretched soldiers but Jesus asked that they be forgiven! I cursed the soldier that held my arms down when they drove the nail through it. I screamed that he rot in Hades but Jesus asked God to bless him. I kicked and screamed when they secured my feet to my cross and I spit at the soldiers. Jesus asked God to forgive him. This man Jesus is known to have performed spectacular miracles and forgive men who have committed the worst crimes against him. This is a special man! This is no ordinary man!

One of the priests yells at Jesus again, "If you are the son of God then come down from that cross! Save yourself! Then... only then will we believe!" Jesus doesn't respond. He hangs in pain; bleeding and gasping for air. Gestas; my cohort from my band of thieves turns toward Jesus and me. He joins the accusations of the priests as he utters his first words toward Jesus. "Jesus! Are you not the Messiah? You are not the son of God! If you are truly the son of God...then save yourself and save us all! Release us from this torture!" Gestas is the fool! This man did nothing to deserve this treatment and punishment! How could Gestas be so foolish as to speak to this man like this?

I turn to Gestas and speak directly to him. "Have you no fear of God? We have been condemned justly, for the sentence we received corresponds to our crimes, but this man has done nothing criminal! He has done nothing wrong!"

I then look into Jesus' eyes. He is looking directly at me. "Jesus, remember me when you come into your kingdom!"

I don't expect a response but Jesus says immediately, "Amen, I say to you, today you will be with me in paradise!"

I cannot fully explain the way I feel at this very moment. My body is in more pain that I could have ever imagined but my heart is so full that I am in tears. Out of all the things that Jesus has to endure, he still takes a moment to tell me that he will not forget me! I will be remembered! I will not be forgotten!

Now I look at the onlookers with a different eye. I look at Gestas with a different eye! I am still in pain. My arms are going numb and I am having difficulty breathing. Yet I am not forgotten! Jesus says that I will be in paradise with him! I don't know what his paradise is but I am joyful that I will leave this pain and torture and be comforted with the Messiah!

Jesus utters a few more words toward the sky and some words toward his mother. I cannot make out what he is saying. I can barely breathe. I push myself higher on my cross which hurts my hands and feet but causes me to get a little air into my lungs. The lack of air is causing me to hallucinate; the sky has immediately turned black. The clouds and sun have disappeared! I must be losing my mind! I'm dying; I'm losing my eyesight and I'm dying!

I look at Jesus and he is slumped over! I look down and soldiers are running frantically! It feels as if the whole earth is moving! The Messiah is dead! Jesus is the Son of God and the earth is shaking because of it! One of the soldiers picks up a club and runs toward Jesus. He is going to break Jesus' legs so he won't be able to push himself up to breathe. He looks up at Jesus and realizes that Jesus is already dead because he does not swing his club. He runs at me and raises his club. He swings it with all of his might and hits both of my legs below the knees. I hear my bones break like glass and I let out the last scream I can muster. My entire body slumps downward as I no longer have the ability to push myself higher on the cross. I can no longer fill my lungs with air and I begin to gasp. Gestas screams as they have just broken his legs as well. The earth is quaking like a pregnant woman laboring her child. I must be dying.

Without air... it is increasingly difficult... to breathe... my head is throbbing as are my hands, feet, back and now legs! Now my... lungs burn within... my chest... I cannot gather enough air... I feel my hands ripping as they cannot uphold the weight... I cannot breathe... I look at Jesus who has just... he has promis... he has given me...paradise...

I take in a breath... I breathe out... I breathe out... I brea...

Darkness.

I open my eyes. The crowd is gone. The high priests are all gone. The crosses are gone. I'm no longer hanging. I feel no pain. I look down at my hands and see light. Bright light. Intense light. Not burning, but bright and marvelous. I look to my side where Jesus was hanging. He is standing beside me, smiling at me. His countenance is like the sun shining in its strength.

I notice that there are others with us. Many others are with us, all shining with the same countenance as Jesus! All magnificent. All intense and bright.

I look ahead of me and see a gate. The bars of the gate are like the bars of a magnificent castle. They look to be made of solid gold. I look in both directions and the gate goes for as far as I can see. I've never seen anything as beautiful. Behind the gate it looks like a garden. The grass is greener than I have ever seen. The path through the gate looks to also be solid gold. Am I dreaming? I have clearly died. Is this the paradise that Jesus promised me? This is breathtaking, not like the loss of my breath which seemed like just moments ago caused me to lose my life.

Jesus and the others approach the gate. I stay close to Jesus and follow his lead. I am still not sure of my surroundings. I have died from my former life. I know that. What this new life is of bright magnificence, I have yet to understand. As we approach the gate, a man steps forward. He is facing us. He is large in stature and holding a staff in his hand. He stretches his hand toward us and begins to speak. His voice is like thunder and it stops us from moving forward. He says "Lift up your heads, O you gates! And be lifted up, you everlasting doors! And the King of glory shall come in. Who is the King of glory?"

This gatekeeper is standing in front of the entrance to the gate. Without hesitation or thought, I open my mouth and answer him. "The Lord strong and mighty, the Lord mighty in battle!"

He asks again, "Lift up your heads, O you gates!

Lift up, you everlasting doors! And the King of glory shall come in. Who is the King of glory?"

I reply along with the others. "The Lord of hosts, he is the King of glory!"

I don't know what made me respond but I do know that Jesus is the Messiah; he is the King of glory! His glory is shining, as are mine and everyone else's. At our declaration that Jesus is the King of glory, the gatekeeper steps aside and the beautiful gates begin to open. We have been granted access with the King.

Since we are all shining and glorified as Jesus is, the gatekeeper asked who is the King of glory. He could not tell which of us is Jesus as we have all been made into his image! We have all been glorified! Now that he is assured that Jesus is amongst us, we are allowed entry into this paradise world that Jesus promised me!

I was a thief. I deserved to be crucified. I committed crime after crime and am not worthy to be with Jesus. He still had mercy on me and remembered me as I asked. Now he is coming into his kingdom and I with him. He gestures toward me to enter the gate and smiles as he says, "Welcome to paradise!"

The Tomb

> "Then he took it down, wrapped it in linen cloth and placed it in a tomb cut in the rock, one in which no one had yet been laid."
> — Luke 23:53

"I am the Tomb!"

I became the most famous tomb in history because of who I was purchased to hold. I am the final resting place of Jesus the Nazarene. Prior to me, the most famous tomb held a man named Lazarus. Jesus' interaction with that tomb made it famous as well.

Lazarus was man who had been dead four days. He was wrapped in grave clothes and laid in the tomb. The mouth of the tomb was sealed by a heavy stone. Many believe that the stone is the heaviest object sealing the tomb when in fact; the spirit of death is what fills every tomb and weighs it down.

Death is a spirit that brings a devastating sting to an individual. When death enters a room, a home, a city, a tomb, its weight is felt. No man recovers from the sting of death. The weight of death is much heavier than the weight of a stone.

Jesus approached the tomb of the dead man, Lazarus and asked that the heavy stone be removed. Many onlookers were surprised at that request.

Lazarus had been dead four days. It is the custom of the Jews that four days is the amount of time necessary to declare an individual dead. Most were unsure what Jesus was going to do. No one thought by moving the stone, Lazarus would walk out. Once the stone was removed, the onlookers were silent. Some expected Jesus to walk inside and pay his respects. Some thought he would anoint the body of the dead man with herbs and spices. Instead, Jesus spoke to the dead. "Lazarus! Come forth!" Within seconds, the dead man walked from the tomb still wrapped in the grave clothes! This was a miracle! The words of Jesus have more weight than the sting of death! He did not have to enter the tomb to defeat the spirit. He simply spoke.

This miraculous event became widespread amongst the Jews. This tomb's popularity grew until it became the most famous tomb in history. The tomb became more famous than the tomb of Moses the patriarch or David the king. The tomb of Lazarus became known all over the world. The man whose words are stronger than death became just as well known.

I am the tomb who will hold his body. I have never held any other body, yet I will hold his. The man who conquered death has now died, and I am to hold his body. He defeated the spirit of death, yet now the sting of death has defeated him. He instructed others to remove the grave clothes from Lazarus, yet now he is being carried into me wrapped in grave clothes.

As the men carry his body inside of me, I await a word. I believe he will wake up and speak. He did it for Lazarus; surely he can do it for himself. Yet he says nothing. His body is as dead as any dead man. There are women weeping as there are at any man's burial. Why did he perform a miracle over another and not perform one to help himself?

After he is placed inside of me, the men who carried him roll a huge stone to seal him in. This stone is heavier than the stone at the tomb of Lazarus. As heavy as it is, I still feel how the spirit of death inside is heavier. The spirit's presence is heavy, as he moves through every inch of the tomb. The spirit holds more weight than the stone. I am now filled with the stench of death, the sting of death, and the weight of death. Jesus is definitely dead.

I was certain that Jesus would perform a miracle. I waited for the supernatural. I strongly desired a word from him, which would alter the circumstance of the present plight. I thought he would speak heavier words than the sting. Instead, I am holding a dead man. Instead of witnessing a champion, I am concealing a corpse. I thought I would see a victor, but instead I am holding a victim. The man who once spoke over death has now been defeated by death…or so I thought.

There is a moment in time where I gave up hope. Doubt overtakes the possibility of the miraculous. The knowledge that he can do it weighs less than the possibility of him doing it. Doubt is a slow, but effective process. I know he has done it before at another tomb. Why not do it again with me? Doubt and the moment clash together in time. Giving up hope and doubt are a pair that meets in time often. In the beginning of the process, one is full of hope and has little doubt. As time progresses, hope fades and doubt grows. If the miraculous expected event does not occur, slowly hope gives way to doubt and they replace one another. One gives up hope and is filled with doubt. This is the exact place I find myself.

Days have passed. No words have been spoken by him. I've felt the heavy spirit inside me since I have been sealed. The supernatural miracle will not happen for me.

This becomes the exact instance a change occurs. When all hope is gone, something happens. When I give up, he shows himself. The first thing I feel is the spirit of death becoming lighter and progressively lighter until I feel the spirit no longer. Next, I feel a bright light and a presence inside me that I have never felt before. It feels the opposite of death. Instead of the sting of death, I feel the love of life.

The love is so overwhelming and strong that it moves the heavy stone from me. The stone was so heavy that it took several men to put it in place. Now it is being moved effortlessly by love. This is a miracle!

And now the one thing I have been waiting for occurs. The supernatural thing that I knew he could do. He didn't do it when I thought he would do it. He didn't do it when I wanted him to do it. Nonetheless, he is now doing it... he is speaking life! As heavy as the stone is, as heavy as death is, as heavy as love is, Jesus' words are the heaviest I have ever felt! He says, "I am the light of the world! I am the door! I am the good shepherd! I am the Son of God! I am the resurrection and the life! I am the way, the truth, and the life! I am the true vine! I am the King of the Jews! All power has been given to me in heaven and in the earth! I have all power in My hand!" Without another word, he walks out.

"O death, where is your victory? O death where is your sting?"

The burial of Jesus Christ

The Cloth

> "Peter, however, got up and ran to the tomb. Bending over, he saw the strips of linen lying by themselves"
> — Luke 24:12

"I am the Linen Cloth!"

I'm specifically referred to as the grave clothes. I dress the dead. A cloth like me is used to wrap a deceased individual, being prepared for burial. I am made of linen which makes me light in both feel and appearance. I am easily removed from a body so the body may be treated with oil and spices after death. If the deceased had been tortured and was bleeding, I am the best material as I will soak up much of the blood.

As I am taken to the body of this crucified man, I cannot believe how bloody he is. Every inch of his body, from the crown of his head to the soles of his feet, is covered in blood. I have to admit that even I was taken aback and had second thoughts about my assignment. With the amount of blood that he has poured out, I may not be able to contain it within my delicate fabric. Nonetheless, I am used and they begin to wrap me around his body.

As I begin to touch him, the effect of the wet blood

causes me to cling to him instantly. I feel his blood move through the very fibers of my fabric. Through the woven intricacies of my makeup, I feel every space within me filled with his blood.

I begin to feel a strength that I have never felt before. It's more than simply the soaking up of blood. There's an unseen power in his blood. There's a quality in his blood that makes his blood different than anyone else's. I can feel it through me. I feel stronger than myself. I feel heavier than my normal weight.

I quickly forget my apprehension about covering his bloody body and replace those thoughts with a new found feeling that I have never experienced. By the time I am covering his entire body, face, and head, I feel so empowered, so strong, so confident.

We're carried and laid on a cold stone slab inside of a tomb carved out of a huge rock structure. This will be his final resting place...this will be my final resting place. I accept my destiny as he accepts his. As the stone closes the mouth of the tomb, the light escapes and the tomb quickly becomes a sea of blackness. Darkness surrounds me and I feel the cold sting of death as it has taken another victim.

I am the grave clothes. I dress the dead. I have fulfilled my purpose. My story ends here.

As I am prepared to spend eternity on this cold slab of stone, it seems like merely a few minutes have passed before something miraculous happens. The dead body that has been covered in blood moves! He begins to wiggle his way loose of my tight grip. Once his hands are free, he begins to pull me off of him layer by layer. This is unbelievable. This is truly miraculous!

Once he has taken me fully off of him, another interesting thing happens. He begins to carefully fold me. As he is folding me, the heavy stone in front of the mouth of the tomb rolls away. Once the stone is removed, he doesn't leave the tomb right away. Instead, he continues to fold me layer by layer until I am as small as a napkin. As he lies me down upon the stone slab that I held him on just minutes earlier, I remember a Jewish tradition. If a Jewish man is served a meal that he enjoys, he takes his napkin and folds it carefully. He lays it upon the table indicating he will be back again. If the man has no intention of returning, he does not fold the napkin. By this man carefully folding me and placing me back down, it means that he is coming back again. He is going to return. I don't know when. No man knows the day or the hour of his return. We do know however that he is definitely coming back.

The women at Christ's grave

Mary Magdalene

"And certain women, which had been healed of evil spirits and infirmities, Mary called Magdalene, out of whom went seven devils."
— Luke 8:2

"I am Mary!"

I am a devout follower of Jesus. My name is so common that I distinguish myself from the other women by using the name Magdalene. I am from Magdala, a town on the western shore of the Sea of Galilee, so most call me Magdalene or Mary Magdalene.

Like many, I had an extremely unique experience upon meeting Jesus. I was a totally different person before meeting him. In fact, it is now hard to remember the woman that I once was.

I remember a time when I followed the customs of the synagogue. I've even spoken to some of the chief priests. I remember the traditions that I learned as a child. Yet somewhere in my youth, I began to go astray. I cannot remember the exact time in my life or the detail of any specific event, but I do know that I lost the desire that I had to follow the law.

What began as a simple stray turned into a complete disregard for the customs of our religious faith. The further I walked away from the right way to live, the easier it became to do what I was doing. This slow process of developing who I would become took years; yet before I knew it, I wouldn't recognize myself anymore.

There are certain acts that I would have never imagined I would commit. There are certain statements I never felt I would utter. There are many thoughts I never felt that I would have. I committed those acts, I uttered those statements and I had those thoughts. I had become an unknown person to myself.

Many of my family members and acquaintances released their bond of friendship with me. For a season, I didn't take notice. I never realized a lack of friends, it's just that the close associations that I had were replaced with a new set of individuals that I was not as familiar with. These new friends were more familiar and closely related with the woman I had become than with the woman that I previously was.

To put it more absolute, I was drowning, yet never realized I had stepped into the ocean.

When I met Jesus, he was unlike any Nazarene or any man I had ever met. The first interaction that we had was very unusual. He looked at me as if he could see right through me. His eyes searched my very soul. I would normally feel self-conscious if someone stared at me, yet I felt safe around Jesus. He approached me and asked a simple question that I will never forget, "What is your name?"

Before I could say Mary or even Magdalene, I utter,

"We were three powers! When my soul had overcome the third power, it went upwards and saw the fourth power, which took seven forms. The first form is darkness, the second desire, the third ignorance, the fourth is the excitement of death, the fifth is the kingdom of the flesh, the sixth is the foolish wisdom of flesh, the seventh is the wrathful wisdom. We are the seven powers of wrath!"

I couldn't believe what I just said! I didn't understand what I just said. I know it was me who said it. It was my voice. It was out of my mouth. I felt the words leave the roof of my mouth. I felt the vibration in my throat when I said darkness and foolish. Yet I became extremely confused. What was I speaking of? I'm not aware or familiar with these statements or terms. Why did I say these things to this man?

Jesus simply looked at me with both piercing eyes and loving eyes. With his next statement, he would change my life forever! Jesus then said, "Come out of her now!" Immediately something changed in me. The desires that I had against the law were gone. The way that I had begun to view life changed. My view changed in an instant. I wasn't sure what happened but I know that something happened. It's almost like closing your eyes during the day and reopening your eyes and it has become twilight in the blink of an eye. A change can occur that swiftly and this is what has happened.

Once that change occurred, I wanted to be near Jesus all the time. I wanted to find out how he was able to change me. I sat with him and listened to him teach. I have never heard someone with such a vast knowledge of the law.

Then I saw him speak to a man. He asked the man the same question he asked me. "What is your name?" I remembered immediately being asked and the strange response and aftermath that I experienced. I wondered if the same thing would happen to this man that happened to me. The man began to weep and hug Jesus. He wanted to follow Jesus as I did.

I later learned the reason for the question Jesus would consistently ask. I learned from his teaching that Jehovah instructed Adam to name the animals in Eden. Whatever Adam said became that animal's name. Adam was created in the image of Jehovah and we were taught that Jehovah is a speaking Spirit. Whatever Jehovah says becomes the law. Whatever Adam said became the name. This is because Jehovah gave Adam the authority over everything. The name of the lion is lion because Adam said so. Jesus would ask a name because he wanted to take authority. Once Jesus knew the name of the spirit, he could take authority because his name is greater than the spirit's name. When Jesus commanded the spirit to flee, the spirit left the person.

This is what happened to me! I had a spirit! Some say I had seven spirits! Jesus took authority and cast them out of me! From that moment on, I have been different. I have been changed. I am even better now than I was before I met Jesus!

All I wanted to do was follow him wherever he went. I wanted to tell others about my experience. I wanted to tell as many as I could that they too should speak with him, listen to him, follow him.

I began to notice however that the chief priests were upset with him. They challenged him with questions. Some spoke very harshly under their breath toward him. Some even shook their fists when he taught. I could not understand why they were angry with him. He never spoke harshly toward them, the law, the temple or the sacred days. He never broke any of the ceremonial laws, yet the keepers of the temple were angry with him constantly.

He angered the Pharisees and Sadducees so much that he was arrested and charged with blasphemy. I had never heard of such an account. I had never heard of a man being brought in front of the council for blasphemy. But Jesus was. I didn't know what to make of it. I didn't know what to think.

Jesus went on trial and was presented to the magistrate. The prefect spoke and uttered the words that even he found no fault in Jesus. I thought that by hearing this, Jesus would be set free. The prefect went so far as to wash his hands from the matter. I knew that Jesus would be released! Instead, the priests paid many in the crowd to cry for the release of another criminal. The prefect had no choice but to release the criminal and judge Jesus. When judgment was announced, I was shocked! Crucifixion!

I immediately began to weep along with Mary; his mother. I could not believe what I had heard! They are going to kill him! Why? He had done no wrong! He hadn't hurt anyone! He hadn't broken any laws! I didn't understand! The man who helped me was now going to be killed!

What I witnessed next was the hardest thing I've ever had to watch. The soldiers tortured Jesus mercilessly. They whipped him and beat him terribly. I thought he would never make it past the beating alive. I've never seen a man beaten before, but I would never think it would be this brutal! I sobbed. I wept. I couldn't look on, but I couldn't tear my eyes away. I could not believe what I was seeing. This kind man... the man who helped me... the man who saved me, was now being ripped to pieces by a lash!

I lost count of how many times the whip slashed him. It seemed to take forever, yet it seemed over in an instant. My mind was racing so fast that it all became a blur. Before I knew it, it was over. There was blood everywhere. He was covered in blood. The whipping post was drenched in his blood. His loin cloth, his hand shackles, his face and hair, were all covered in blood. Was there any blood left in his body? Could he even stay alive long enough to be crucified? He couldn't even walk! How would he be able to go on?

By the time I saw him again I felt that I had no more tears to cry. I felt so numb, it was as if I was suspended in time and witnessing a dream. Jesus was now wearing thorns on his head that were causing him to bleed. His head was now bleeding. There was blood pouring across his face, into his eyes, dripping from his chin. How could someone be so cruel as to put heavy thorns into his head?

Jesus is now carrying a large wood structure. He, along with two other men who are to be put to death as well, is carrying wood. They were not beaten as badly as Jesus was. They were not bleeding as he is now. He was still made to carry the weight of this wooden structure while he was beaten half to death and his head was pouring blood. Yet he still managed to look in my direction and catch my glance. He looked right through me like he did when I first met him. The same eyes, the same piercing glance as when we met. The difference now though is he didn't ask my name, he didn't say a word. I felt no guilt as before. I felt no condemnation. It seems as if he managed to smile before being pushed to move on with the cross structure.

The crowd has gathered to witness his death. There are so many people; pushing and shoving, screaming and yelling. I can't hear myself think. Sometimes the pushing gets so intense that the Roman soldiers step in to calm people down. Sometimes the crowd is so thick that I lose sight of Jesus. I have to hurry through so many people to keep up. I never lose sight of the wood he is carrying though. I can see it as he tries to labor forward.

By the time Jesus arrives at the top of the hill, he is exhausted from carrying the wood and from being beaten so badly. I am exhausted from crying... caring... loving... hurting... feeling for him.

They nail him. I don't even want to look at him. I turn toward the crowd as to not have to look at how grotesque Jesus' body and face have become. I see the scribes and Sadducees that taunted him. I remember the Pharisees and I see most of them. Some are quietly watching. Some are mocking him. Some scream "He was able to save others! Now he cannot save himself!" I want to run up and scream and quiet this mob! I want to tell them how he changed me. I want to explain how he healed me and he never blasphemed. I want to tell them how I saw him treat children with kindness and teach in the town. I want everyone to love him as I love him. The words cannot form in my mouth to help him. I am speechless as I see him agonizing and trying to breathe. I want to help him because he helped me. I love him. I want to die as well but I can't. I can only stand and witness them killing him.

    I feel like I cannot breathe. The more I attempt to capture air into my lungs, the quicker my breath seems to come, yet it is not satisfying. This seems like a nightmare that I cannot wake up from. I have no voice, I have no energy. I have tried to scream but nothing comes forth. I've held my head in my hands; I've wiped my eyes on my tunic. I've coughed. I've prayed. I have nothing left. I'm devastated. I'm tired. I'm exhausted. I'm crushed.

    Jesus looks up to the sky and says something aloud. I cannot understand what he is saying. Then as if in slow motion, his head falls. His eyes close and his body goes limp. He is dead. The crowd is hysterical as the sky has suddenly turned dark. It feels as if the ground is moving. None of that matters. Some have lost their balance and fallen down. Some have begun to run. None of that matters. His mother, John and I approach the cross. We had not been allowed to come this close because of the soldiers. Now the soldiers are running. I want to see him one last time.

Jesus is dead and there is still blood dripping from his body. I look up at the man who changed my life; the man who saved me. Now he is dead. He saved so many others; why didn't he save himself?

The events over the next hours and the next days are a blur to my memory. I don't remember it all. I do know that I did not sleep. I do know that I barely consumed food or water. The little I did eat gave me a sick feeling in my stomach. I still can't believe I will never see Jesus again. I will never hear his voice or hear him tell stories again. I will never see him perform the unusual miracles I witnessed. So many people were touched and changed as I was. This will never happen again.

When I was asked to assist in the anointing of his body, I readily accepted. I am not sure how I will feel when I see his lifeless body again, yet I have to go. I have to help anoint and clean him. I have to go.

I watched the men carry him down from the cross. I watched them wrap him in the linen cloth of the dead. I went to the burial place with Joseph and the others. I saw the men roll the stone to shut the mouth of the tomb. I do not know who will roll the stone away today, as there are only two other women accompanying me to anoint him. Such matters seem trivial when thoughts consume me of him. Little has mattered as I try to get through these days without crying myself sick. Who will open the tomb for us? Who will close the tomb for us? I don't know. None of us do. Maybe the soldiers will assist us. But when has a Roman ever assisted a Jew?

In the distance, as we approach, it seems as if the stone is in a different position than it was when we left. I quicken my pace, as do the others. As I thought, the stone has been rolled away! I cannot feel my feet as I begin to run inside the tomb to see if his body has been tampered with. Maybe someone else is here to anoint him. My worst fear is that someone has stolen his body. I immediately begin to cry as I draw closer to the open sepulcher.

I'm afraid to enter the tomb and confirm my fear. I look inside and see two men; one standing where his head was laid and one standing where his feet were. His body however is gone. One of them speaks to me directly. "Woman, why are you weeping?"

"They have taken away my Lord and I do not know where they have laid him."

I turn to see a third man standing behind me. I suppose him to be the gardener. He must have been the one to remove the body and hidden it somewhere else. He must be returning from taking the body away. "Sir, if you have carried the body of Jesus away, tell me where you have laid him, and I will take him."

He looks at me as if he could see right through me. His eyes search my very soul. I would normally feel self-conscious if someone stared at me, yet I feel safe. He approaches me and says my name. "Mary!" It is Jesus! How? Am I dreaming? Am I seeing a ghost? He isn't clothed in linen or covered in blood. His countenance seems bright and his voice is reassuring as it always is. I did not recognize him by glancing at him when I turned around, but that voice! I know it is him! "Teacher!" I proclaim.

I rush to embrace him but he forbids me. "Do not cling to me, for I have not yet ascended to the Father; but go to my brothers and say to them, I am ascending to my Father and your Father to my God and your God."

I am overwhelmed with joy! I cannot wait to share the news with the others! I immediately run from the tomb with the other women to find the men in hiding! What news to share! What good news! As I am running, the thought comes to me... I was such a wretched person. I was so far from the law and from God. I should have been condemned to die for I was the guilty one! Yet Jesus changed and saved me! Now, of all the people that he could have chosen to appear to first, he chose me! He could have chosen John for we all know that he loves John. He could have chosen Lazarus for we all witnessed him weep over Lazarus. He could have chosen Peter as he seems to have taught Peter so much over the last few years. He could have chosen Nicodemus whom he taught to be born once more. He could have chosen any of these men who have followed him, yet he chose me! He actually chose me! He will need me to spread the word that he is alive! He is back and alive!

No matter how low I felt or how badly I had done, Jesus still chose to use me. If he can use a person with a past as I have, then I am sure he can choose to use anyone! I'm sure he can. I'm sure he will.

The Resurrection of Jesus Christ

The Stone

"He rolled a big stone in front of the entrance to the tomb and went away."
– Matthew 27:60

"I am the stone!"

I sealed the tomb that Jesus the Nazarene was buried in. Once Jesus was crucified, his body was placed in the tomb and Joseph of Arimathea rolled me in front of the cave opening. I am a weighty stone. I am a heavy stone. I cover the final resting place. I seal the dead and confine them to their earthly fate.

This Jesus who has been crucified has caused quite a stir in town. There have been debates, arguments, meetings, plots as well as adoration and loyalty to this man. Although my role is merely to seal his final resting place, I cannot help but to be intrigued by him. What is it about him that has the entire town in an uproar? There are those who hate him as passionately as those who love him. There are those who fear his movement and some who follow his movement. Everyone has an opinion and it is a strong one. What manner of man is this? Is it simply because he said that he is God's son?

As they carry his body inside the tomb, I cannot get a good look at him because he is wrapped in grave clothes. I want to see what is so special about him.

I want to know what makes him unique. Is he truly special or just an ordinary man from Bethlehem?

He is placed inside the tomb and those that have come have paid their last respects. After everyone has exited the tomb, I am rolled to the mouth of the cave opening and set in place. Once settled, I fit securely into the opening. I am set in place and not easily moved. It would be impossible for women to remove me from outside the tomb and equally impossible for Jesus to remove me from inside the tomb. No man would have the strength or the leverage to remove me, especially not from the inside.

As the first two days have passed, I can't help but to ponder this man from Galilee. There was such a great following, yet most of his disciples are in hiding and not visiting the tomb. There is a Roman soldier assigned to make sure the body is not taken yet there have been no tomb raiders or individuals wishing to remove him.

On the morning of the third day, something very unusual happens. I feel myself shifting and releasing from the mouth of the cave. Since I fit into the mouth of the cave, I have begun to settle in. Yet now, I am being pushed... from the inside. I don't feel hands on me from the inside, but something is causing me to unplug the cave opening. I begin to move, yet no one is touching me. I begin to roll but no one is pushing me. There is a force causing me to move but I cannot see it.

It is at this point that I remember a story I heard of Jesus. There was a time when he sent his disciples ahead of him in a boat. He wanted to stay behind to pray and he promised to meet them on the other side. As they ventured out to sea, the winds and the waves grew strong. The men had great difficulty maintaining their boat in the midst of the storm. This is when the miraculous takes place. The men look out to sea and notice what they think is a man walking toward them on the water. It can't be a man though, for it is impossible to walk on water. No man has ever done it before; no man will ever do it. The disciples become deathly afraid for they deduce that it must be a spirit coming toward them. It has to be a spirit, it cannot be a man. It isn't until Jesus assures them that it is indeed him and to not be afraid that they recognize that it is indeed Jesus.

How can he walk on water unless he truly is the son of God? He has to be the son of God, for no man can walk on water. Yet, another interesting thing happens. Peter, one of the twelve, asks Jesus if he too could walk on water and join Jesus where he stood. Jesus told him to come and Peter immediately steps out of the boat! Peter begins to walk on the water toward Jesus! Peter is not the son of God, so how is he able to walk on water as well? This is impossible and Peter begins to realize it. When the reality sets in that he is walking on water, and the waves and wind are still very strong, he panics and begins to sink. Jesus catches him and asks him why he lost his faith.

Why has he lost his faith? His faith. Walking on water seems to be a matter of faith. Impossible acts becoming possible seem to be a matter of belief. Jesus says "All things are possible to him that believes." Jesus says "I tell you the truth, if you have faith and don't doubt, you can do things like this and much more. You can even say to this mountain, 'May you be lifted up and thrown into the sea, and it will happen.'" If that type of belief can move a mountain, it can certainly roll a stone from the mouth of a cave opening!

    As I begin to roll away from the tomb, I gain a deep respect for this man Jesus. He has once again done the impossible. Can a dead man get up and walk again? Jesus has done the impossible! Can a heavy stone be rolled away from a power inside of a tomb without human hands touching it? Jesus has done the impossible! Through the power of his resurrection, he who believes can do the impossible as well! Through faith, a believer can do the impossible! All things are possible to him that believes! Jesus has afforded the believer the power to do the impossible just as he did with Peter. All one must do is have faith and believe.

The Angels at the Tomb

"For God commands the angels to guard you in all your ways."
— Psalm 91:11

"I am a Guardian Angel."

I'm one of the angels assigned to Jesus. All angels are ministering spirits and we all have assignments. From the three chief regent Archangels to the heavenly bodies, we all have assignments.

The three Archangels were Michael, Gabriel and Lucifer. They each had individual assignments.

The Archangel Michael's assignment is warfare. He is responsible to fight and protect on God's behalf. When Moses died, Satan wanted to take his body. Michael contended with Satan over the body of Moses. Satan laid claim to the body because Moses murdered an Egyptian but Michael fought on God's behalf. What an honor to guard the body of God's servant, Moses! God needed Moses to speak with Jesus along with Elijah on the mountaintop so his body had to be preserved. His body had to be protected because it would be used again. Michael is a warrior. This is his assignment.

The Archangel Gabriel's assignment is prophecy. He speaks to humans on God's behalf. Gabriel interpreted many of Daniel's dreams and gave him the prophetic understanding of his visions. He also prophesied to both Elizabeth and Mary when they became pregnant. Elizabeth carried John the baptizer and Mary carried Jesus, the anointed One. This was his assignment.

The Archangel Lucifer's assignment was worship. Lucifer was made of music. I remember when he was referred to as the morning star. Job even says, "When the morning stars sang together, and all the sons of God shouted for joy." It was even prophesied about him that the workmanship of his timbrels and his pipes were prepared in the day that he was created. He was made of music. His sound was perfect harmony. When he moved, he created worship. He directed the angelic host in a beautiful arrangement. He worshiped God in the beauty of God's holiness. This was his assignment.

There are angels known as Seraphim. These angels have an assignment. They are the caretakers of God's throne. They continuously sing His praises. "Holy, holy, holy is the Lord of hosts. All the earth is filled with His glory." This is their continual chant as they fly around his thrown. These angels are assigned to do this and it is their love and zeal for God which drives them to pursue their assignment.

There are angels known as Cherubim. These angels are beyond the throne of God and are the guardians of light and of the stars. Their assignment is to protect things outside of the realm of the throne room. A mighty Cherubim was selected to guard Eden when Adam and Eve were cast out.

Every angel has an assignment and all angels take their assignment seriously. Lucifer even took his assignment seriously and led worship with great diligence before he made his decision to ascend higher than the throne of God. Lucifer exuded music, praise and worship. It came out of his pores. It was in every sentence he spoke. He loved to worship because that was his God given assignment.

When Jesus fasted in the wilderness, he was tempted by satan. After Jesus endured the temptation, there were angels that were assigned to minister to him. What an honor! What a privilege! God has to have such faith in His ministering angels to allow them to guard and protect His Son.

Jesus once said that He had the authority to call upon his Father and have twelve legions of angels dispatched on his behalf. These are angels assigned to him. To be amongst this group is indeed an honor. Many angels are simply awaiting an instruction to serve, for they are willing to take their assignment seriously.

When Jesus' final days on earth had passed, there came an angelic assignment to guard his body. His spirit had been committed into the hands of his Father, but his body had to be buried and kept. His body had to be protected because it would be used again, just like in the days of Moses.

I was chosen. Of the legions of angels that could have been selected, I am one of two that was chosen. What a privilege and an honor! My assignment is to protect Jesus' body while it lies in the tomb. I do not know the amount of time of my assignment. I do not know the end result for his body. I do know that I will protect his body at all costs. I will take this assignment seriously for I have been dispatched by God.

It is very difficult to determine how long I have been guarding the deceased body for I normally do not exist in time. God is eternal, which means that He is timeless. He is not limited by the portal of time that He created for humans. I exist in the heavenly realm with God so I am not used to time. This assignment has dropped me into the time realm and I have had to get used to counting hours as humans do. Humans count hours on a daily basis. Angels do not count hours. In the time portal, there is a past, a present, and a future. In eternity where God and the angels are, there is just I Am.

From the moment I assumed my post, it has been close to seventy-two hours. It has been three days that I have stood watch. I do not know the length in human time of my assignment but I am prepared to guard for three thousand times three thousand human years. I am fortunate to be chosen and I do not take my selection lightly. I am prepared to count the hours until human hours end. So far I have counted seventy-two.

As I prepare to begin counting the minutes starting the seventy third hour, the hand of Jesus' dead body moves. Startled, I jump and quickly scan the tomb for demonic activity. There is none. As I turn back toward his body, his left arm reaches across his entire body and starts to pull the grave clothes. I stand motionless as does the other angel. Then everything stops. No motion, no movement. His left arm is draped across his chest.

I look at the other angel and he looks back at me. Neither of us know what to say or act upon. If there is demonic activity present and there is an attempt to take his body, I will fight. God will send legions of angels if He has to. God will send Michael if He has to! I will fight alongside Michael and the angels who have committed to warfare for the King!

The body moves again, this time sitting up! He can't fully sit up for the grave clothes are still tight but now both arms begin to tear the cloth. First he rips from the face and head, then the arms. In my shocked state, the only thing I can do is jump to assist. The other angel quickly begins to assist as well. Neither of us can clearly define what is happening but it seems as if the body has life! The body that has been dead and cold for three days now has life! He has been motionless and now he is tearing off the grave clothes!

We begin to help. We are furiously tearing the wrapping off of him as his head becomes uncovered. Still in a state of shock, I stop for a moment to look at him. He smiles at me and says, "Peace be still." Immediately I drop to my knees to worship him.

"Holy! Holy! Holy are you Lord! Both heaven and earth are filled with your majesty!"

As the graves clothes have loosened, he sits up more comfortably and places his hand on my head. "All power has been given to Me in both heaven and earth." He says, "I have made all things new."

Through his hand, I feel a power I have never felt before. He has such strength that he imparts when he anoints. I've felt and experienced it. Even his glance has power. There seems to be power in his resurrected body.

Suddenly the tomb illuminates with the brightest light. A glory shines around Jesus like the glory in the throne room of heaven. At the exact time the tomb fills with light, I hear the stone at the mouth of the tomb begin to move. The heavy stone begins to roll from the tomb as if it is as light as angel's wings.

The early morning sunlight from outside now spills into the tomb a little at a time as the light from Jesus slowly fades. He stands and begins to remove the rest of the grave clothes from his body. The linen that he was draped in now falls to the floor. He picks the linen off the tomb floor and neatly folds it together. He places it down in the spot where he was lying just moments ago. He seems very careful to place it down neatly. He walks toward the opening of the tomb and turns back to look at us. Jesus gives us that piercing, yet loving look. He gives the glance that has power. His eyes are strong and his smile is warm, genuine and inviting.

Without another word, Jesus turns and walks out of the tomb... resurrected. His body was needed for him to live again!

Cleopas

"That very day two of them were going to a village named Emmaus, about seven miles from Jerusalem, and they were talking with each other about all these things that had happened. While they were talking and discussing together, Jesus himself drew near and went with them."
— Luke 24:13-15

"I am Cleopas!"

"This is the saddest time I have ever experienced in my life. I have never experienced such loss at any point."

"Neither have I," says my companion. "In the history of Jerusalem, never have such tragic events taken place than what we have witnessed."

"Do you remember the time when he spoke about the children? Remember how he embraced them and blessed them all one by one?" I asked.

"Yes I do Cleopas! Yes I do! This is one of the reasons I was certain he would restore Israel. I thought that he was looking to our children as the future leaders of the restored kingdom. I was always amazed when I listened to him speak but it was even more profound when he was around the children. I felt like a child when I sat at his feet. He spoke so eloquently regarding the kingdom that I also felt he was going to restore Israel to its rightful place under God. He spoke with such authority about God and the kingdom. He had to be the son of God to know as much as he knew. But why would God's son allow himself to be crucified as he has?"

This is the very question I have asked myself! Maybe his claim was not true. Maybe he wasn't who he said he was. If he was from God, why didn't he fight back and destroy all those who opposed him? Remember the story of how God destroyed the army of Pharaoh as he was pursuing our forefathers in the wilderness? If our God has always destroyed the enemies of his people, why would he allow his son who has come to redeem us to be killed so horrifically?

Another man joins my friend and I, as we are walking along. I am not familiar with this gentleman but he is walking in the same direction we are toward Emmaus. I can tell by the way he greets us that he is Jewish as we are. I have to apologize to him for my sad demeanor. It's the impact of what has happened over the last three days that has me in a state of shock.

"Sir, I am sorry if I appear to be saddened. My friend and I were just discussing and questioning the sad state of affairs that our people have found themselves in from the events over the last few days."

"What communications are these that you have one with another?" he asks.

"Have you been by yourself in Jerusalem over the past few days and not know the things which have taken place?"

"What things?" he asks.

"What things? The things concerning Jesus the Nazarene who was a prophet, mighty in deed and word before God and all the people. The chief priest and our rulers delivered him up to be condemned to death and have crucified him. We had a rich hope that it was he who should redeem Israel. Today is the third day since these things came to pass and certain women of our company amazed us today. They went to the tomb early this morning to anoint his body with oil and fragrances. When they arrived, they found that the large stone was rolled away from the tomb and his body was missing. They told us that they saw a vision of angels who said that Jesus was alive! So we hurried to the tomb and found it just as they had said. We fear someone has stolen his body for neither we nor the women earlier saw him."

"Oh foolish men! Why are you slow of heart to believe in all that the prophets have spoken? The Christ had to suffer these things to enter into his glory. Do you not know that Moses was a prophet of God and he received instructions to build the tabernacle in the wilderness? The high priest entered the tabernacle once each year carrying the blood of the sacrificed lamb into the Most Holy place. This process is the foreshadow to the Christ as he is both the high priest and the sacrificial lamb. Not with the blood of goats and calves but with his own blood he entered the Most Holy place once for all having obtained eternal redemption. For God our Father spoke to both the prophet Moses and his brother Aaron with the instructions that no bone shall be broken of the Passover lamb. In the same manner, no bone was broken of the Christ when crucified. Do you not remember being told that the Christ is the Passover Lamb? Did not Moses also teach us as a prophet the things concerning Him who was to come? He taught that 'If a man has committed a sin deserving of death, and he is put to death, and you hang him on a tree, his body shall not remain overnight on the tree, but you shall surely bury him that day, so that you do not defile the land which the Lord your God is giving you as an inheritance; for he who is hanged is accursed of God.' Jesus, who you speak of, said that He would become a ransom for the sin of the world. He carried sin to the cross and hung on that tree yet was buried in the same day as the prophets foretold."

He continued, "The book of the prophet Joshua in its entirety is a prophecy of the spiritual conquest through Jesus the Messiah. In the book of the prophet Nehemiah, Joshua is written as Yeshua, the name for Jesus. Indeed, the book of Joshua in the Greek Septuagint Old Testament is entitled Jesus. Both Joshua and Jesus mean the same; the Lord saves."

I became amazed at this stranger's words. He spoke eloquently and with authority as a learned man of the religious order.

"The high priest Pinchas was also a prophet and he foretold of the coming Christ. Don't you remember that God sent a plague because his people intermingled with the Midianites of the Promised Land? Pinchas thrust a spear through Zimri and Cozbi who were the offending couple. God our Father noticed that Pinchas showed loyalty and bravery for him. God decided not to destroy all of the children of Israel in anger because Pinchas had made atonement for their sins. God declared that Pinchas and his sons for all eternity would receive divine recognition for this; a covenant of peace and the covenant of an everlasting hereditary priesthood. This is a prophecy to the Christ who came and suffered as He too made atonement for the sins of the people, creating an everlasting covenant between God and man. There is also Elkanah the father of Samuel. He indeed was a prophet. Although many men did mistreat their barren wives in that day, Elkanah did the opposite: he comforted, elevated, loved and had compassion on his wife Hannah. Rather than despising and rejecting his wife after the worldly manner, Elkanah respected and submitted himself to the will of God to make his wife barren; and instead loved his wife as Christ loves the church. He showed the example of Jesus who was to come in the manner in which he dealt with his bride. Did he not foretell the coming of the Christ and how he would suffer for the sake of the church?"

My friend and I are speechless as we listen to the various prophecies given about Jesus. The stranger continues.

"Look at the comparison of the prophet Samuel and Jesus the Christ. Samuel was born to a woman who otherwise would not have had children. Hannah was barren. The Christ was born to a woman who otherwise would not have had children yet for Mary was a virgin. Samuel was the firstborn son of his mother. Jesus was the firstborn of his mother. Samuel was given to the Lord all the days of his life. Christ was given to the Lord all his life. Samuel grew up serving amidst the wicked priests of Israel. Jesus grew up among hypocritical scribes, Pharisees and the corrupt Sanhedrin. Samuel hid none of the things from Eli the priest that God has said against and concerning Eli. In the same manner, Jesus hid none of the things from the chief priest that God the Father said against any of them.

    Samuel as a prophet was the foreshadow to Jesus the Christ as he witnessed how Israel rejected God our Father as their true king and wanted a man instead. Jesus was in like manner rejected as king of the Jews when they cried out that they wanted Caesar as their king. 'The Lord has searched for a man after His own heart and the Lord has commanded him to be captain over His people.' These are the words spoken by the prophet Samuel in the hearing of King Saul. Was he not prophesying about the coming of the Christ whom the Lord sought after and made him captain of his people? After these things came the prophet Nathan. The prophet spoke in the hearing of King David these words; 'When your days are fulfilled and you rest with your fathers, I will set up your seed after you, who will come from your body, and I will establish his kingdom. He shall build a house for My name, and I will establish the throne of His kingdom forever. I will be His Father, and He shall be My son.' Is not Jesus the Christ the Seed of David?"

    "Yes he is!"

    "And King David himself spoke prophetically of the Christ who was to come when he said 'The Lord has said to Me, you are My Son, this day I have begotten you. Ask of Me and I will give you the nations for your inheritance and the ends of the Earth for your possession.' Did he not also say regarding the Christ 'The Lord said to my Lord, Sit at My right hand, till I make your enemies your footstool...?' Of whom could he have been speaking of but the only begotten of the Father? David's son King Solomon sat on the throne of Israel after David rested with his fathers. King Solomon spoke by wisdom of Jesus when he said 'Who has established all the ends of the Earth? What is His Name, and what is His Son's Name if you know?' Solomon wrote that by the Spirit of the Lord concerning Jesus who walked amongst you, taught you and broke bread with you. Do you remember? Can you recall what he said to you concerning the things that were to come? Do you see how he fulfilled all that was said concerning the Christ?"

"Yes!"

"And did not the prophet Obadiah write, 'The day of the Lord is near for all nations. As you have done, it will be done to you; your deeds will return upon your own head. Just as you drank on my holy hill, so all the nations will drink continually; they will drink and drink and be as if they had never been. But on Mount Zion will be deliverance; it will be holy, and Jacob will possess his inheritance.' Do you remember how Jesus said that He had come that all would have life more abundantly? The prophet says that all will drink upon the holy hill now that the Christ has come. All nations shall partake in that which the Lord has done through His only begotten Son! Other prophets spoke on him as well. While the prophet Hosea wrote, 'When Israel was a child, I loved him, and out of Egypt I called My son.' The prophet Amos wrote, 'And it shall come to pass in that day that I will make the sun go down at noon and I will darken the Earth in broad daylight; I will turn your feasts into mourning, and all your songs into lamentation; I will bring sackcloth on every waist, And baldness on every head; I will make it like mourning for an only Son, and its end like a bitter day.' Think back to the day in which Jesus was nailed to the cross. Was it not a bitter end? Did the sky not turn to darkness and the Earth quake like a woman in labor? Did not his people mourn and lament over him? Did Amos not rightly prophecy that day and what was to come concerning Jesus? Has Jesus the Christ not fulfilled the words written in the scriptures by the prophets before him? Are you aware of the prophet Micah and what he wrote foretelling Jesus the Son of God? 'But you, O Bethlehem Ephrathah, though you are little among the thousands of Judah, yet out of you shall come forth to me the One to be Ruler in Israel, whose goings forth have been from of old, from everlasting.' Do you remember what tribe Jesus comes forth from?"

"Yes! Jesus is of the tribe of Judah!"

The stranger looks directly at me. His eyes are glaring right into mine as he asks me very directly if I was in attendance when Jesus spoke to the scribes and Pharisees who asked to see a sign or miracle. I certainly was in attendance and recall that day as if it were yesterday.

"When asked by the scribes and Pharisees to show

a sign in order to prove that he was the Son of God, Jesus replied, 'An evil and adulterous generation seeks after a sign and there shall no sign be given to it but the sign of the prophet Jonah: For as Jonah was three days and three nights in the whale's belly; so shall the Son of man be three days and three nights in the heart of the earth.' Did Jesus spend three days and three nights in the tomb before this day in which you have given testimony that his body is no longer in the tomb?"

"Yes! Yes he did!"

"Jesus came to fulfill the words that each of the prophets said about him. He did that in your hearing and in you walking with him. Did he not fulfill every word of the prophet Isaiah? Isaiah wrote, 'Behold, the virgin shall conceive and bear a Son, and shall call his name Immanuel.' Was not Jesus born of a virgin? Do you also remember that the prophet Isaiah wrote, 'The people who walked in darkness have seen a great light; those who dwell in the land of the shadow of death, upon them a light has shined.' Were you there when Jesus read the words of the prophet Isaiah from the scriptures? Jesus read 'The Spirit of the Lord God is upon me, because the Lord has anointed me to preach good tidings to the poor; He has sent me to heal the brokenhearted, to proclaim liberty to the captives, and the opening of the prison to those who are bound; to proclaim the acceptable year of the Lord, and the day of vengeance of our God; to comfort all who mourn.' Jesus then stated that the very scripture was being fulfilled in their hearing! Do you remember?"

"Yes! Yes, I was there! Everyone was silent as Jesus

closed the book and took his seat! We were all amazed at how he read from the prophet's words!"

"The prophet's words were fulfilled!" the stranger says. He continues, "The words of the prophet Habakkuk; 'Look among the nations and watch, be utterly astounded! For I will work a work in your days, which you would not believe, though it was told you.' This is fulfilled by Jesus this very day! Jesus taught his followers many things concerning the kingdom of heaven and that he would suffer many things. How many of the followers believed what he said? How many are sad as you are this day yet remember what he told them? How many believe on him yet doubt him in times of trouble? How many understand his words and deeds yet fear grips their hearts when persecution arises?"

These words were cutting yet true! I followed Jesus' every word and deed. I believed in him. Yet now that persecution has come, do I not believe any longer? When I heard of this miracle of his body being gone, did I believe or did I doubt? Is it easy to believe at times of peace and comfort but harder to believe when problems arise? My heart is burning as this man walks and talks with us!

"Jesus is foretold in the words of the prophet Jeremiah; 'Behold, the days are coming, when I shall rise up for David a righteous Branch; and he will reign as King and act wisely and do justice and righteousness in the land. In his days Judah will be saved, and Israel will dwell securely; and this is his name by which he will be called, the Lord our righteousness.' This is who Jesus is! These words have been fulfilled!"

As we draw close to the village of Emmaus, I do not want this man to cease talking with us. I wish we had further to walk so we can continue to hear him speak on the fulfillment of scripture through Jesus whom we knew.

"Hear the words of the prophet Zechariah in which he writes in the scripture; 'Rejoice greatly, Oh daughter of Zion! Behold, your King is coming to you; he is just and having salvation, yet he is lowly and riding on a donkey.' Do you not remember him coming into Jerusalem riding on a donkey? Do you not remember how the people received their king that day? What a joyous celebration yet he was lowly and riding on a donkey. Did not the prophet Zechariah also write 'So they weighed out for my wages thirty pieces of silver and the Lord said to me, 'Throw it to the potter' that princely price they set on me.' What was the amount that Jesus was betrayed for?"

"Thirty pieces of silver!"

"The prophet Malachi wrote, 'Behold, I am going to send My messenger, and he will clear the way before me. And the Lord, whom you seek, will suddenly come to his temple; and the messenger of the covenant, in whom you delight, behold, he is coming.' Was not John who baptized in the river the messenger who came before Jesus?"

"Yes!"

"Are the prophet Malachi's words fulfilled in your hearing through the life of Jesus?"

"Yes! Every word written! They have indeed been fulfilled through His life!"

"Look, we have arrived at the village," the stranger says. "I see the lights from the homes in the near distance. It has been my pleasure accompanying you and speaking with you. I am traveling further than Emmaus."

I cannot allow this gentleman to travel further. He spoke so eloquently with us. He spoke with such clarity and authority as a man who is truly learned of the scripture. It is late in the day and he is certainly welcome to abide with us for the evening. It would bring us great pleasure if he could continue speaking with us regarding the things pertaining to Jesus while at supper. Sir, abide with us for it is toward evening and the day is now far spent.

"Yes, I will abide with you. Thank you." he replies kindly.

I knock on the door and our friends open. They welcome us in and we introduce our new found friend. He is greeted with warm smiles and salutations. It is almost supper time and the women are preparing the table and the meal. We invite our guest to sit and we sit after him.

"We were on our way and discussing the events of the last few days. As we were walking and talking, this kind gentleman joined us and began to share with us his thoughts on the fulfillment of the scriptures as it pertains to Jesus who we followed. If he would be so kind, maybe he would share with the rest of us some of the things he shared along the journey here. He spoke of so many of the prophets and how they foretold of Jesus."

"I would be very interested to hear this!" someone proclaimed.

I found myself as amazed with this man as I was when I would listen to Jesus speaking. Jewish leaders purposely asked him questions that they felt would trap him by his very answer. Instead, he would find a way to answer and confuse the leader who asked. This man that I met only today has impressed me in the same manner. He spoke as a learned man with a thorough understanding of the scriptures and the prophets of old. As it was with Jesus, I can sit at this man's feet and hear him speak for hours.

The meal is placed in front of us. As everyone is seated for the meal, the man takes the bread. "Father, it was Your good pleasure and for Your glory to make this day and as you have blessed us, I ask that you bless this meal that we are to partake in." He then breaks the bread in half. Immediately, I remember eating a meal that Jesus had with us! The prayer he prayed before the meal was "Father, it was Your good pleasure and for Your glory to make this day and as you have blessed us, I ask that you bless this meal that we are to partake in." He then broke the bread and began to pass it out to those sitting with us. I looked at his face closely and realize it is Jesus! I am speechless! I feel like my heart has stopped! I am so excited that I am overwhelmed and in another second, Jesus vanishes! Jesus disappears! He is gone! There is a large gasp in the room! Everyone drew a huge breath because of the shock of his immediate disappearance! Everyone begins to look at one another in shock! No one has said a word! We are all in a state of shock!

Was not our heart burning within us, while he spoke to us in the way, while he opened to us the Scriptures?

I smile, which turns into smiles around the household. Jesus is alive! Jesus walked and talked to us on the road! He is alive! He chose to walk and talk with us! Jesus taught, he loved, he died but now he is alive! Most of all, Jesus did what he said he would do; he fulfilled the words of all the prophets!

Thomas

"Then he said to Thomas, 'Put your finger here, and see my hands; and put out your hand, and place it in my side. Do not disbelieve, but believe.'"
– John 20:27

"I am Thomas!"

I am one of the men who followed Jesus. Many believe I followed him because he asked me to. That may be the case with some of the brothers, but not with me. I followed Jesus because he captivated me. I had never met anyone who drew such attention. He was not afraid of soldiers. He spoke directly to the temple priests and seemed to know more of the law than they did. Jesus was captivating.

When I met Jesus, his words began to stay with me. He spoke about a kingdom but he wasn't a king. He instead was a carpenter. I continually asked myself how he could speak as he did with such authority. I asked myself how this man from Galilee could challenge the political establishment of both Rome and Jerusalem. When he spoke, the crowds would be filled with men who either believed what he said, thought he was mad, or were spies for the priests. I chose to be one who believed. Between his words, the amazing things I saw him do, or just his persona, I gave him my loyalty.

I quickly abandoned all I had ever known. I left my home and profession to follow him. I knew that my family would not understand my decision but at the same time, I knew that they didn't understand him. I've witnessed the Romans strike fear in my people. I've even watched my father cower before them at times of census. I've seen a man arrested and beaten as the soldiers took him from his family. When I saw Jesus stand up for what he taught, I knew he must have been the Messiah. I left everything I had ever worked for and gained in life without hesitation.

I grew to be fully engrossed in his message and his character. I was ready to die for him. I remember when we were in Judea and many of the Jews sought to stone him. They were accusing him of blasphemy and had picked up large stones to hurl at him. We were able to escape, yet the image of the mob never left my mind. Some of them were so angry that they clinched their teeth together and shook their fists at us. Some of the priests cursed him strongly. No matter what Jesus said to answer their questions, they would not be appeased. They had set it in their hearts to stone Jesus and his followers. We were able to escape but many of the brothers trembled with fear.

The next significant event would solidify my devotion to Jesus beyond what I could comprehend. Our friend Lazarus was sick unto death. His sisters; Mary and Martha came to us to give us the news. Everyone knew that Jesus had the power to heal those who suffered from illness. We remember when Jesus healed the nobleman's son in Capernaum. He was sick unto death as well. With one word, Jesus healed that young man. Jesus didn't even leave to attend to the young man. He spoke the right words and the young man was healed in that seventh hour. When Mary approached Jesus to tell him about her brother, we thought Jesus would once again speak a word to heal Lazarus. Jesus didn't respond to the news. Jesus didn't speak the healing words nor respond as to what he was going to do for two full days.

After the second day, Jesus spoke to us saying that he wanted to return to Judea to see about Lazarus. Judea is the city where we were almost stoned. I knew some of the brothers would rather Jesus speak the healing words where we were instead of traveling back. Some of the brothers even mentioned to Jesus that we should not go back. I didn't agree with them. I've seen Jesus win every debate against the Sadducees and the scribes. I've even seen him speak with authority to the Pharisees. I spoke up directly to my brothers; "Let us also go, that we may die with him!" I felt brave and bold. I knew that I had sold everything to follow Jesus. I had no choice but to fully submit to him because I had given everything else away. I knew he could heal Lazarus. I knew he wanted to heal Lazarus. If that meant stoning, then let us die with him!

What I witnessed over the following two days amazed me. Lazarus had died from his sickness. Jesus did not speak the healing words to deliver him, nor did we travel to Judea right away. Jesus finally arrives at the tomb where they had laid Lazarus after four days. In our culture, four days is the minimum amount of days when a person dies until he is declared legally dead. Lazarus was definitely dead, wrapped in grave clothes, and placed in a tomb. The family was in mourning as we approached and some confronted Jesus for not healing him. Jesus was not bothered by their words or cries. Instead, he began to cry. I have never seen Jesus weep. I have never seen him show vulnerability like this. He must have loved Lazarus for he cried for him. Then he asked for them to remove the stone from the opening of the grave where they laid him. I had no idea what Jesus was doing. Maybe he wanted to see his friend's face one final time. Maybe he wanted to pray to his Father for the soul of Lazarus. None of us were aware of what would happen next.

Once the stone was removed, Jesus called Lazarus to come forth and everyone was shocked as they witnessed Lazarus walking from the tomb. Lazarus walked out of the tomb! He was bound from head to toe in his grave clothes! Jesus had brought a dead man back to life! I didn't believe it! I, as well as the others, was amazed! I would never doubt him! He is the Son of God! He has to be! Who else has the power over death to raise a man from the dead?

From that point on, Jesus' popularity grew. Everywhere we went; crowds would press to get to him. He had single handedly turned Jerusalem upside down as he continued to challenge popular opinion. At the same time, the hatred toward him grew more intense. It seemed that there were spies and members of the Pharisee class on every corner. Their challenges grew to be more intense. Their responses to his statements drew more fury. They were looking for anything in the law that would allow them to kill both Jesus and all of his followers. The people loved Jesus, but the ruling class of priests seemed to hate him.

I remember distinctly when Passover season approached. Jesus had given us instructions to prepare the Passover meal and that he would celebrate with us. As we were eating, Jesus made a very unusual statement. "One of you shall betray me." He said it so confidently that it silenced the entire room. At first I heard murmurs and whispers. Then one of the brothers asked Jesus if it was him. Then another... and another. As confident as I was in my loyalty to Jesus, I have to admit that I asked as well. I don't know what would have ever caused me to betray or lose my belief in Jesus. By this point, I had witnessed too much to doubt him. We all breathed a sigh of relief when Jesus said that it would be Judas. Admittedly, I did. I don't know what reason Judas would have to betray him. I know that I had no reason to. I didn't think much of the incident once Judas left the room.

After that night, things began to unravel. Judas did betray Jesus and led the guards and Pharisees right to him. When news began to spread that the priests and guards had finally arrested Jesus, we were shocked. No one knew what to do. James and John told us what happened in the Gethsemane garden. Jesus was beaten severely as they took him. None of us wanted to be arrested and beaten yet we did not know what to do without his leadership. We went into hiding. We awaited word from him on what he wanted us to do. I didn't know if he was going to speak a mystical word to free himself or have us fight to free him. He had never been arrested before. Each time the Pharisees came for him, we managed to slip away. This time was different. Peter, James and John were with him but they couldn't defend him. They allowed him to be taken. Some of the brothers were angry at them for that. I wasn't. I simply waited patiently for the message from Jesus. I knew he would tell us something.

The first word that we received was that he would stand trial. Although it seemed as if he was falsely accused, he would still stand trial for counts of blasphemy, treason, and other crimes. I was growing anxious as to what Jesus would do. I believed he had the power to free himself. I knew he would speak one word and be free; so for that, I waited.

The next day, I was surprised to learn that he had already been convicted and condemned. Many alleged criminals wait months in confinement before they are tried. Jesus, on the other hand, was tried and convicted in a single day. Surely at this point he will speak one word to set himself free. Maybe he will get a message to Peter, James or John. Maybe he will send instructions to one of his brothers or to Mary. None of us know what to do and none of us want to be seen. We know that the same fate awaits us and no one wants to face that.

He is set to be crucified. He has already been beaten very badly. The message that I heard is that the Romans were allowed to whip him within an inch of his life. I don't understand how he showed so much authority and power before and now is allowing them to beat, ridicule, and taunt him. I remember when he fed the huge crowd of people with the fish and bread. I was amazed that everyone was able to eat and we had baskets of abundance left over. Now that I think back to that event, maybe he didn't multiply the food as I thought. Maybe he merely broke off very small fragments. If he cannot free himself from the soldiers, maybe he is just a man like I am. I remember when he turned the water into wine at the wedding in Cana. Maybe he really didn't change it. Maybe the guests were so filled with wine that they didn't realize that it was merely water. If he cannot free himself from the prison, maybe he is just a man like I am. I remember when the storm was so fierce that I thought the boat that we were in would tip over. I was sure we would drown. We woke Jesus up and he calmed the sea. Maybe the wind was subsiding anyway. Maybe the waves were calming anyway. If Jesus cannot save himself from being tortured by soldiers, maybe he is a mere man like the rest of us.

    For the first time since meeting Jesus, my belief begins to lessen. It seemed as if everything was happening so fast. I didn't have time to think straight. I now think about the life that I left behind. What am I to do now? I left everything to follow Jesus. I quit my job. I left my father's house. I followed Jesus' teaching and now don't have a teacher. I followed his guide and am now left alone. Now what? I became numb. I was speechless from shock, as well as not having the words to conjure. How could this be? So many things began to run through my mind. I now have to go back home. I now have to face the critics and cynics who listened to my reasons for following Jesus. I have to tell them that they were right. I have to come to terms with the fact that Jesus was nothing more than a man as I am. I have to explain to myself how he was able to perform miracles in my life. Everyone in Jerusalem has seen me with Jesus. They will arrest me and crucify me next! I have to be alone to decide what I will now do.

The message came to me that the brothers were going to meet. I was anxious to learn what our strategy would be. Would we move to a new city together and start over? Would we take up new careers and try to rebuild our lives? Do we take our families on our journey or leave them behind? Do we approach the ruling council and beg for forgiveness? When I arrived at the room, it was refreshing to see my brothers enter. Bartholomew and Phillip. James and John. Peter. Matthew. Surprisingly though, as each man entered, they expressed excitement and joy. They hugged one another. Some openly wept. I grabbed one of the men to learn what the excitement was about and he told me that he saw Jesus. He told me that Jesus was alive. The next man proclaimed the same thing, as did the next man.

I wanted to know if the fellows had been drinking or hallucinating. Jesus is dead and buried in a tomb. How can they claim to have seen him? There was so much talking and excitement that I couldn't hear myself think. I loudly quieted the room to hear the full claim. "Thomas! We have seen him! We were assembled here and he appeared to us! Just as you and I are standing here now! He was here! We all witnessed it! He spoke with us! He ate with us! He is alive!"

"This is crazy! Brothers, this is crazy! Jesus is dead!

You all know it to be true! I know this is difficult to believe. I am having a difficult time as well but he is dead. We followed him to no avail! Jesus is dead! He was beaten, bruised, tortured, and crucified. He is not living, he is dead!"

Each man speaks trying to convince me that Jesus was truly alive. Some grabbed me and shook my arms. Others tried to quietly reason with me. Some became agitated with my disbelief. Nevertheless, I would not believe this outlandish claim. Unless I see the print of the nails in his hands and place my hand into his side where he was pierced, I will not believe!

The days that followed were more of the same. They were filled with my brothers and the women trying to convince me, but presenting no evidence other than their witness. They asked me to think back to the miracles. I tried my best to explain each one. From the water being turned to wine... maybe the guests were too drunk to notice mere water. To the healing of the blind beggar... maybe he could see all along and was faking. My frustration level grew as did theirs. I had had enough. I didn't want to hear any further of this mystical claim. Days had passed and I had no reason to believe. My belief had left me homeless. My belief had left me without a career. My belief has ostracized me from my very family. I simply refuse to go back and become a believer.

Eight days after the tragic end to my teacher, mentor, and friend, we had gathered again to decide what to do next. We were in the room with the door securely shut and locked. All of the brothers were there except of course Judas who had met a tragic end himself. The next thing that happened would change my life forever. Without warning or announcement, Jesus appears in the room. He didn't come through the door, he was just there. Some screamed from shock while others fell to their knees. Jesus smiled and approached me as if I was the only person in the room. He walked past John, his beloved. He passed Peter, who he said he would build his church on. He passed Matthew, who had the horrible job of collecting taxes. He passed both the sons of Zebedee who wanted to sit on Jesus' right and left side. He walked directly to me and smiled. He opened his arms wide and spoke the words that I will never forget.

"Thomas. Come and take my hands to see the print of the nails. Place your finger into the print of the nails. Take your hand and place it into my side to see where I was pierced. Do not be without faith, but believe."

"My Lord and my God!" That was all that I could say. "My Lord... and my God!"

"Thomas, because you now see me, you believe. Blessed are those that have not seen me, yet believe."

I fell into his arms and wept upon his shoulder. I was rendered speechless once again. I looked around the room and my brothers simply smiled at me. No one was condemning. No one ridiculed me for not believing. They were simply happy that all of my doubt has been erased.

This is amazing! Jesus defeated death and the grave! Not only that, but he entered the room that had a securely locked door. What is most amazing is that he knew what I had said about him without physically being there! He knew what I said about touching his hands. He somehow knew what I said about placing my hand into the wound in his side. I am amazed and will forever follow his lead. Jesus is Lord and I will preach him confidently from now on! I believe and will never doubt my Lord Jesus again!

The risen Christ appears at Emmaus

Two Men in White Robes

> "And while they were gazing into heaven as he went, behold, two men stood by them in white robes, and said, "Men of Galilee, why do you stand looking into heaven? This Jesus, who was taken up from you into heaven, will come in the same way as you saw him go into heaven."
> — Acts 1:10-11

"I am a witness!"

We established the final words of Jesus to the men of Galilee. When Jesus spoke with them on that day, I knew it was his final time with his followers before he left the earth. They did not know that he would leave them as he did. They were asking about the kingdom and would it be restored back to Israel. As they asked these questions, we realized that many of the things Jesus said and did were misunderstood.

Many of the followers of Jesus thought that he would restore Israel to a place of dominance. Many waited for a military revolt to do this and thought that Jesus would be the leader of the revolution. It wouldn't be until much later that his words would resonate in the spirit of the true believers and make sense to those who have an ear to hear. Peter didn't understand a lot of what Jesus taught until long after Jesus returned to heaven. This is when Peter's true ministry began.

Whether or not a believer understands immediately or later, the Word must be established. The Lord said in his Word that out of the mouth of two or three witnesses, every word shall be established. So as I stood by the men of Galilee on that day, I was prepared to witness to what Jesus was saying and what he was going to do.

As they had gathered, one spoke and said "Lord, are you at this time going to restore the kingdom to Israel?" Jesus replied, "It is not for you to know the times or dates the Father has set by His own authority. But you will receive power when the Holy Spirit comes on you and you will be my witnesses in Jerusalem, and in all Judea and Samaria and to the ends of the earth." Jesus' body slowly begins to levitate into the air right before them. Everyone standing is speechless. No one moves a muscle. They were witnessing a miracle! This man Jesus began floating in air! The higher he ascended, the more they gazed on. No one said a word. As he entered the clouds, we lost sight of him. He had finished his work and returned to his rightful place in the throne room of heaven.

Our task now is to speak and seal what he promised them. He promised his believers that he would return. Several times while on earth, Jesus spoke of his return. "For as lightning that comes from the east is visible even in the west, so will be the coming of the Son of Man. At that time the sign of the Son of Man will appear in the sky, and all the nations of the earth will mourn. They will see the Son of Man coming on the clouds of the sky, with power and great glory. No one knows about that day or hour, not even the angels in heaven, nor the Son, but only the Father. As it was in the days of Noah, so it will be at the coming of the Son of Man. For in the days before the flood, people were eating and drinking, marrying and giving in marriage, up to the day Noah entered the ark; and they knew nothing about what would happen until the flood came and took them all away. That is how it will be at the coming of the Son of Man. Therefore keep watch, because you do not know on what day your Lord will come." There are many occasions when he spoke words such as this. Some had an ear to hear, others didn't. Some misunderstood, others received at that time. The Word still has to be established in the mouth of two or three witnesses.

I, along with the other witness am dressed in white robes. The men had not paid attention to us for they were focused on the miracle of Jesus floating away. As they gazed into the sky, our charge came forth. Now is the time to seal the Word from the Lord.

"Men of Galilee, why do you stand looking into heaven? This Jesus, who was taken up from you into heaven, will come in the same way as you saw him go into heaven."

The men were glad to receive our report. They remembered what Jesus had said to them about his triumphant return. Now that the witnesses have spoken, every believer can rest in knowing that he will return in both glory and majesty! Amen.

The risen Christ appears to his disciples

Epilogue

To the reader, you may have noticed the use of the lower case letter "h" throughout *Conversations of the Crucifixion* in reference to Jesus (he, him, his, etc). In most theological manuscripts, the letter "h" is capitalized to show the respect the Lord Jesus deserves in referring to His person. In this book, many of the objects or individuals speaking did not recognize who He was. In their minds, He was simply another carpenter, teacher, or radical leader. It wasn't until it was revealed that they grew a greater respect for Jesus and His purpose.

As to not confuse the reader, I did not change from lower case to upper case in those instances where they realized who He was. Subsequently, you may notice a lower case s in the name Satan. Many theological texts will not give the respect of a capital letter to his name even though it is the grammatically correct thing to do.

Lastly, you may notice the tense changes (past or present) throughout the book. Some of the objects or individuals were speaking before the crucifixion took place. Other objects or individuals were speaking during the crucifixion. The final set of objects or individuals speak after the crucifixion.

As the crucifixion of the Lord Jesus Christ is one of the three most significant events in human history, (the birth and resurrection of Jesus being the others), *Conversations of the Crucifixion* centers on the event of the crucifixion. An object or individual's perspective is based solely on when and how they relate to the cross.

Thank You

Thank you Father God, thank You for the gift of writing, a skill You have deposited into me without me earning it or deserving it. I love you Lord, thank You. Thank you Jesus for saving my soul. Thank you Holy Spirit for speaking to me and guiding me and for helping me to write this book.

Thank you to my wife Kathy for allowing me to stay up night after night to write and for always being supportive and encouraging of what I love to do. Big thanks to my baby boy Dylan who is the reason I am focused and writing. Thank you for bringing the joy of fatherhood to my life.

Thank you to Bishop Don D. Meares, my senior pastor. You have taught me to pursue my destiny in God and given me the liberty to do so. Thank you so much Bishop. Thank you for the words on the back of this book that you provided "...with pleasure!"

Thank you to Elder R. Kevin Matthews for the idea of *Conversations of the Crucifixion*. You trusted me to write it for the dramatic presentation and this book is the fruit of that labor. Thank you for always preaching encouragement to me. I cannot tell you what your mentorship means to me.

Thank you to Minister Kevin Williams who first believed in me as a writer and allowed me to work on So How Ya Livin' Now and From the Hood to the Hill: The Next Generation.

Thank you to Rev. Maurice Nutt, my fraternity brother and encourager. Thank you for the words in the foreword you provided and for always supporting my work.

Thank you to my parents James and Bertha Gourdine who are always supportive of my dreams and aspirations.

Thank you to my brother Darnell and his wife Timika, and my niece and nephew Zarria and Jackson. Darnell, thanks so much for your photography skills in both my picture for this book and the images on the DVD. Thank you also for the awesome promotional pieces you created for the book!

Thank you to my sister Stephanie for always having my back.

Thank you to my writing partner and soror, Lynnette R. Barrett for editing this book and for being such a great friend over the years. Your keen eye and attention to detail were critical in the perfecting of this work. I cannot thank you enough.

Thank you to Marja Humphrey for being a spiritual eye over this project and for your timely advice and counsel.

Thank you to Victoria Fleary for your awesome design of the book cover and subsequent pieces for this work! Love ya Sis!

Thank you to Norman Rich for the layout of this book, the *Conversation of the Crucifixion* study guide, and the building of the website. I appreciate all of your hard work and effort.

Thank you to my cousin Reggie Dupree for working on the digital downloads to all of my books. I cannot tell you how much I appreciate you doing this for me man!

Thank you to my cousin Jason Gourdine of Crown Vision Media for the outstanding work you did in creating the Conversations of the Crucifixion DVD. You have such a bright future ahead of you and I can't wait to get started on some of our upcoming projects!

A big thank you to all of my fans who have supported my work over the years: As the Sands Burn, Beyond the Burning Sands, The Saved and the Restless, Jewels: The Story of the Founding of Alpha Phi Alpha Fraternity and Jewels: The Story of the Expansion of Alpha Phi Alpha Fraternity. It's because of all of your emails and words of encouragement that I continue to write. Thank you to each of you.

And a special thank you to the person holding this book and reading it right now. I hope you have been blessed by this narrative of the most important event in human history; the death, burial, and resurrection of Jesus Christ. If you don't know Him as Lord and Savior, accept Him into your heart now. He went through everything detailed in this book because He loves you and wants you to accept Him as Lord. To do that, it is very simple. The Bible states in Romans 10:9, If you confess with your mouth that Jesus is Lord and believe in your heart that God raised him from the dead, you will be saved. Take the time to do this if you never have and get to know Him as Lord. It will change your life for the better! Get connected to a bible teaching church in your area and begin to walk in the full joy of God's love! He came and died that you could have eternal life. Accept it and live it!

I would love to hear from you! If this book has impacted you, taught you something, caused you to reflect on the crucifixion in a new way, or most importantly led you to make a decision for Jesus Christ, I would love to hear about it. Write me at darrius@crucifixionconversations.com and share your testimony!

God bless you richly and mightily!

Darrius Jerome Gourdine

Made in the USA
Charleston, SC
07 April 2014